▶ **The Golden Dawn's 'Nationalist Solution'**

DOI: 10.1057/9781137535917.0001

Reform and Transition in the Mediterranean

Series Editor: **Ioannis N. Grigoriadis**

Dr. Ioannis N. Grigoriadis is Assistant Professor and Jean Monnet Chair of European Studies in the Department of Political Science and Public Administration, Bilkent University, Turkey, and Research Fellow at the Hellenic Foundation for European & Foreign Policy (ELIAMEP), Greece. His research interests include European, Middle Eastern politics, nationalism and democratization. His recent publications include *Instilling Religion in Greek and Turkish Nationalism: A "Sacred Synthesis"* (2012) and *Trials of Europeanization: Turkish Political Culture and the European Union* (2009).

The series of political and economic crises that befell many Mediterranean countries has renewed scholarly attention on this important region. This series aims to provide a venue for the comparative study of reform and transition in the Mediterranean within and across the region's political, cultural, and religious boundaries. In an effort to explore the structural conditions of reform and transition, as well as the interrelations between politics, history, and culture in this volatile region, the series draws on interdisciplinary approaches, including perspectives from political science, history, sociology, economics, anthropology, and area and cultural studies.

Titles include:

Sofia Vasilopoulou and Daphne Halikiopoulou
THE GOLDEN DAWN'S 'NATIONALIST SOLUTION'
Explaining the Rise of the Far Right in Greece

DOI: 10.1057/9781137535917.0001

palgrave▸pivot

The Golden Dawn's 'Nationalist Solution': Explaining the Rise of the Far Right in Greece

Sofia Vasilopoulou
University of York, United Kingdom

and

Daphne Halikiopoulou
University of Reading, United Kingdom

palgrave
macmillan

DOI: 10.1057/9781137535917.0001

THE GOLDEN DAWN'S 'NATIONALIST SOLUTION'
Copyright © Sofia Vasilopoulou and Daphne Halikiopoulou, 2015.

All rights reserved.

First published in 2015 by
PALGRAVE MACMILLAN®
in the United States—a division of St. Martin's Press LLC,
175 Fifth Avenue, New York, NY 10010.

Where this book is distributed in the UK, Europe and the rest of the world,
this is by Palgrave Macmillan, a division of Macmillan Publishers Limited,
registered in England, company number 785998, of Houndmills,
Basingstoke, Hampshire RG21 6XS.

Palgrave Macmillan is the global academic imprint of the above companies
and has companies and representatives throughout the world.

Palgrave® and Macmillan® are registered trademarks in the United States,
the United Kingdom, Europe and other countries.

ISBN: 978-1-137-53590-0 EPUB
ISBN: 978-1-137-53591-7 PDF
ISBN: 978-1-137-48712-4 Hardback

Library of Congress Cataloging-in-Publication Data is available from
the Library of Congress.

A catalogue record of the book is available from the British Library.

First edition: 2015

www.palgrave.com/pivot

DOI: 10.1057/9781137535917

Contents

List of Illustrations

Figures

Tables

DOI: 10.1057/9781137535917.0002

Series Editor's Preface

Acute economic and political crises are usually positively correlated with the rise of political extremism and anti-systemic political movements. This has been confirmed in the context of the European sovereign debt crisis, which has contributed to the rise of far left and far right parties throughout the European Union. Nevertheless, it is only in Greece that this crisis has led to the emergence of a sizable neo-Nazi political party. The 'Golden Dawn' moved from the fringes of Greek politics and 0.29 per cent of the vote in the 2009 elections to 6.97 per cent in the May 2012 elections. This has sent shockwaves across Greece and beyond, not least because of the fact that Greece was one of the European countries hardest hit by German occupation in the Second World War. Despite public outcry and the arrest of its leading political cadre for their involvement in multi-fold criminal activities, the party has been able to form a solid electoral support base that has voted for the party in the June 2012 parliamentary elections and the May 2014 European elections. The 'Golden Dawn' phenomenon has fuelled the debate about 'Greek exceptionalism' in the context of the European crisis and invited scholarly discussions about its permissive conditions in Greek political culture and society. This book by Dr. Daphne Halikiopoulou and Dr. Sofia Vasilopoulou comprises a timely and enlightening scholarly contribution to the study of one of the most vexing dimensions of the Greek economic and political crisis.

Acknowledgements

This book reflects years of research on far right politics and on the Golden Dawn more specifically. It is the product of a long-standing collaboration and co-authorship.

Versions of the arguments and materials presented in this book were initially published in other outlets. Certain sub-sections of Chapter 2 were initially published in *South European Society and Politics* (2013, 18(4): 523–542). Other sub-sections of the same chapter were first published in Giusto, H., Kitching, D. and Rizzo, S. (eds.) (2013) *The Changing Faces of Populism: Systemic Challengers in Europe and the US* (Brussels: Foundation for European Progressive Studies). Finally, sub-sections of the conclusion were previously published in 'Political Instability and the Persistence of Religion in Greece: The Policy Implications of the Cultural Defence Paradigm' (2013), RECODE Paper Series, Augsburg: European Science Foundation, ISSN 2242–3559. Some of the overall ideas and themes published in the book first appeared in the LSE EUROPP blog. We are grateful for permission to reproduce these materials.

The arguments put forward in this book have been reformulated to reflect methodological challenges. For their support and input, we thank John Breuilly, Katjana Gattermann and Marco Steenbergen. We are grateful to Margarita Markoviti for assisting with the coding of a large number of Golden Dawn materials. We thank the University of York for granting financial support to make this coding possible.

DOI: 10.1057/9781137535917.0004

Needless to say, all errors and misjudgements are entirely our own.

Both authors have contributed equally to this book. The order of names reflects the principle of rotation.

DOI: 10.1057/9781137535917.0004

palgrave▶**pivot**

1
Introduction

Abstract: *This chapter sets out the rationale and themes of the book. The chapter first contextualises the Golden Dawn and defines it as a far right, and more specifically fascist, party. It then proceeds to examine the broader theoretical framework on the rise of far right-wing parties and movements, discussing demand- and supply-side dynamics. The chapter concludes by presenting the main argument of the book, which focuses on the interdependence of these dynamics and, in particular, what we term the Golden Dawn's 'nationalist solution' to an overall crisis of the nation-state in Greece.*

Keywords: crisis; far right; Golden Dawn

Vasilopoulou, Sofia and Daphne Halikiopoulou. *The Golden Dawn's 'Nationalist Solution': Explaining the Rise of the Far Right in Greece*. New York: Palgrave Macmillan, 2015. DOI: 10.1057/9781137535917.0005.

The fall of fascist regimes in the years following the end of the Second World War marked the de-legitimisation of right-wing extremism across Europe. The ideas of radical authoritarian nationalism associated with Mussolini's Italy, Hitler's Germany, Franco's Spain and Salazar's Portugal have become progressively discredited, paving the way to democratic ideals and the predominance of representative institutions over authoritarian statism. Those societal groups and parties associated with 'old' fascist traditions including anti-Semitism, anti-communism, and anti-systemic principles, as well as connections with the inter-war right, have been in progressive decline precisely because of their nostalgia for fascist ideals. Increasingly on the other hand, the far right-wing parties that are successful in Europe are those who have been able to modernise their ideology, framing the debate in terms of civic principles such as democracy, citizenship and respect for the rule of law. These parties distance themselves from fascism, often rejecting the far right label and denounce violence.

In Greece in particular, fascist ideals have been unthinkable, not least because of the memory of the Nazi invasion in the 1940s and the atrocities and deprivation that followed, as well as the country's own experience of military dictatorship in the 1960s and 1970s. And yet in May and June 2012, over 400,000 Greek citizens voted for a party that represents precisely those ideals that are so vilified in Greece. The Golden Dawn (*Χρυσή Αυγή*) received 7 per cent of the vote in May and 6.9 per cent in June, granting it 21 and 18 parliamentary seats out of 300, respectively. It managed to retain its support in the 2014 European Parliament Elections receiving 9.38 per cent of the vote, despite its association with a large number of violent acts, which resulted in the imprisonment of the majority of its MPs, including the party leader in 2013/2014.

The Golden Dawn is an extreme, ultra-nationalist, and racist party. Among current far right-wing parties in Europe, it is the one that most resembles fascism, and in particular Nazism, in its outright espousal of National Socialism: the endorsement of what it terms the 'third biggest ideology in history', that is, nationalism, combined with support for an all-powerful state premised on 'popular sovereignty' (Golden Dawn 2012b). The party's logo is the Greek meander, which is reminiscent of the Nazi swastika. Its guiding two-fold principles are blood and honour. The first is defined in racial terms and the second in moral terms as the supreme ethical value. This captures the essence of its Nazi ideology. Since its election, the Golden Dawn has been careful in its public espousal of the

DOI: 10.1057/9781137535917.0005

Hitlerite regime. Although in the past it has made declarations glorifying the 'enlightened leadership of Adolf Hitler' (Psarras 2012: 40), the party has also been quick to argue that Nazism is case-specific, that is, the type of National Socialism as applied to Germany alone, and therefore it is inappropriate to speak of a Greek variant of Nazism. However—albeit this rhetoric—the espousal of National Socialism can hardly be disassociated from Nazism on ideological grounds.

First, the party emphasises white supremacy and equates the state with ethnicity. Its ideology centres on the Greek nation, which it understands as an organic entity defined by ethnic identifiers. These identifiers are confined to biological and cultural elements, such as bloodline, language, religion, and community of birth, making the Greek nation an exclusive club to which membership is restricted. There is a clear line of delineation between members and outsiders. Greek status cannot be acquired; it is something one is born into. As such, racism informs the party's policy agenda. The Golden Dawn is staunchly and indiscriminately anti-immigrant, emphasizing that there is no such thing as 'legal' immigration. During its electoral campaign in June 2012, many of its members declared that immigration can never be legal; the party manifesto promised that if elected the party would expel all immigrants from Greece. In the same manifesto, the party denied the granting of full political rights to any non-Greek—as defined by the biological features described earlier—on the grounds that granting Greek citizenship to non-natives will 'spoil' the continuity of the Greek nation (Golden Dawn 2012d: 5).

Second, the Golden Dawn resembles fascism in terms of its rejection of communism and liberalism, which it describes as tyrannical (Golden Dawn 2012d: 1). The party identifies middle-class complacency, liberal democracy, and communism (Breuilly 1993) as the 'enemies from within': the key sources of internal threat to the nation. This explains its anti-systemicity and rejection of substantive democracy. The party denies the 'far right' label, which it argues equates it with other 'traitor' far right parties that have accepted the path of parliamentary democracy (Fragoudaki 2013: 55). It opposes democracy on a number of grounds; for example, that it cannot be applied in practice; that it was not actually approved by the ancient Greeks; and that it gives power to any layman who may not endorse nationalist ideals. Third, the party is a militant organisation defined by violence, discipline and ultimate respect for the leader to the extent that party members are required to stand and

DOI: 10.1057/9781137535917.0005

salute upon the leader's arrival. Its members define themselves as street soldiers. Some, including its leader, have authored monographs, which tend to glorify violence.

Since the Golden Dawn's establishment as a bulletin in 1980, its members have been consistently involved in the perpetration of violent acts. They have targeted people because of their ethnic background—as external enemies—and their political persuasion—as internal enemies. Examples of ethnically motivated violence are numerous, including attacks against Turkish and Kurdish refugees, immigrants of African origin, and Albanian immigrants on a large scale during the 1990s. The party has continued to be involved in violence against immigrants, following its election in 2012, and has been linked to many incidents of hate violence, including the murder of Shezhad Luqman in 2013. Its members are renowned for targeting market vendors, small shop owners of non-Greek origin, and manual workers. The majority of incidents have occurred in public spaces (squares, streets and public transport) and involved physical attacks, beatings, and stabbings. There have also been incidents of arson and property damage.

Notorious cases of political violence include the perpetration of grievous bodily harm against student members of mainly left-wing groups, including attacks against members of the Communist Youth of Greece (*Κομμουνιστική Νεολαία Ελλάδας*, KNE) throughout the 1990s and the attempted murder of left-wing student Dimitris Kousouris in 1998. More recently, the murder of left-wing activist Pavlos Fyssas, also known as Killah P, in Athens in 2013 triggered the arrest of 20 or so Golden Dawn MPs and members for their involvement in and management of a criminal organisation. Those arrested included the leader of the Golden Dawn, Nikos Michaloliakos; prominent MPs including Elias Kassidiaris, Nikos Mihos, Elias Panagiotaros and Ioannis Lagos; and a number of police officers. They faced a series of charges, including Fyssas's murder; the murder of a Pakistani immigrant in Athens a few months earlier; two attempted murders against immigrants; several beatings and incidents of grievous bodily harm; and blackmail and money laundering. The authorities were also concerned with accusations with regard to the recruitment of children in accordance to Nazi practices. Many of these cases were brought to public attention in 2014, during the preparation of the case file against the Golden Dawn (*Kathimerini* 2014).

Despite its extremism, the Golden Dawn is one of the most successful far right-wing parties in the Greek post-dictatorship era and certainly

DOI: 10.1057/9781137535917.0005

the one whose ideology most resembles radical authoritarian national- ism. The arrests and the events that followed revealed the extent of the problem. Instead of weakening Golden Dawn's support, the crackdown and imprisonment of its MPs had the opposite effect, with the party maintaining its support as third party in the 2014 European Parliament elections. The timing of the arrests also begs the question of why these did not take place earlier. The murder of Pakistani immigrant Shezhad Luqman only a few months before failed to generate such a response. It was a violent act against a Greek citizen that prompted the authorities to act. In addition, the party's presumed links with the army and the police brought to the forefront the question of the impartiality of what is the only source of organised and legitimate violence in a state.

What has facilitated the rise of an extreme, ultra-nationalist party such as the Golden Dawn in a country that has experienced Nazi invasion and a military dictatorship? This book seeks to explain the rise of the Golden Dawn by understanding the party itself, its ideology, strategy, and voting base. We propose an explanation that, taking into account complex economic and political dynamics, focuses on a party strategic response to societal crisis. Starting from the premise that the economic crisis that Greece experienced was all-encompassing, with significant political and ideological implications, we term the Greek crisis as an 'overall crisis of democracy and the nation-state'. We understand the rise of the Golden Dawn within the context of high levels of disillusionment, dissatisfac- tion with democracy, and electoral volatility. Within this context, we examine the Golden Dawn's strategic response to the crisis in terms of the offering of a 'nationalist solution' through the employment of two fascist myths in its discourse: the myth of social decadence and the myth of national rebirth. It is through these two myths that the Golden Dawn promises the dispossessed an escape from their social, economic and overall human desolation.

Understanding the rise of the far right

The 'far right' is an umbrella term used to describe a broad range of social groups, movements, and parties across Europe whose core ideological doctrine is nationalism (Eatwell 2000). These groups are also defined by anti-immigration attitudes, authoritarianism and anti-establishment populism (Hainsworth 2008). The diversity of this party family has

DOI: 10.1057/9781137535917.0005

created debate within the discipline regarding the correct label to characterise parties belonging to it, including 'extreme right', 'radical right', 'neo-populist right', and 'far right'. In this book, we adopt the term 'far right' as a more generic one to describe social groups, movements and parties that belong to both the 'extreme' and 'radical' right categories. The distinction between the extreme and radical right is a distinction of kind, referring to a party's relationship with democracy and violence. While the extreme right rejects both procedural and substantive democracy, the radical right accepts procedural but rejects liberal democracy (Mudde 2010). Carter (2005) defines 'right-wing extremism' as encompassing a rejection of democratic principles and human equality. Extreme right-wing parties tend to be associated with fascist principles and ideals and may maintain connections with the inter-war right. Radical right parties tend to disassociate themselves from fascism and define 'otherness' in accordance to ideological rather than racial and bloodline criteria (Halikiopoulou et al. 2013).

The Golden Dawn belongs to the extreme right category of the broader far right label both because of its stance on democracy and because of its espousal of fascist, and more specifically Nazi, ideals. Its key values, actions and, power organisations fulfil Mann's (2004) criteria of a fascist group including nationalism, statism, paramilitarism, transcendence, and cleansing. It may also be described as fascist in terms of its negations: it is 'anti-bourgeois, anti-liberal and anti-Marxist' (Breuilly 1993: 290). The Golden Dawn's key goal is to transcend social cleavages internally and cleanse the nation ethnically by eliminating external enemies. It accepts violence as a legitimate means of doing so. The party differs from other authoritarian rightist movements and parties in Greece in that, similarly to Nazism, it rejects elitism and sees itself as a popular mass movement from below. The leader of the party aspires to be the leader of the nation embodying the singular will of the masses. The Golden Dawn's ultimate goal is full control of state power in the name of the nation.

Explanations for the rise of the far right may be categorised in terms of demand (Lipset 1960; Bell 1964; Adorno et al. 1969) and supply (Koopmans and Statham 1999; Mudde 2010; Halikiopoulou et al. 2013). Demand-side explanations associate societal crises with the rise of the far right. The main assumption here is that societal crises significantly alter the insecurities, expectations and preferences of those segments of the population that are more vulnerable to socio-economic changes. These citizens are more likely to express their dissatisfaction by opting for a

DOI: 10.1057/9781137535917.0005

far right-wing party. Such explanations may be psychological (Bell 1964; Adorno et al. 1969), class-based (Lipset 1960) or cleavage-based (Kriesi et al. 2006). They see the far right as an undesirable part, rejection of or alternative to modernity (Eatwell 2001). The inter-war economic crisis and the wide social discontent it generated have been closely linked with the rise of Nazism and Fascism in Europe (Lipset 1960). According to Mann (2004), fascism was the result of four simultaneous crises: economic, political, ideological and military. Fascists 'were generated in large numbers by post-war crises in ideological, economic, military, and political power relations to which a transcendent nation-statist ideology spearheaded by "popular" paramilitaries offered a plausible solution' (Mann 2004: 365). The far right became an option by offering a solution at a time when it seemed 'impossible to alleviate political, social, or economic misery in a manner worthy of man' (Arendt 1951: 459). This solution was effective because it 'bridged the ideological schism of modernity' (Mann 2004: 365).

Supply-side explanations are top-down. As radical right-wing parties progressively substituted those with a fascist past in European political arenas, and experienced increasing support at times not necessarily linked with severe economic or political or ideological or military crises, scholars turned to supply as a way of understanding this new phenomenon. These explanations are institutional and focus upon opportunities for parties, whether they are posed by the political system itself (political opportunity structures—POS) or created by the party through organisation and rhetorical strategies (discursive opportunity structures—DOS) (Mudde 2007). POS focus on party competition and party system dynamics. Such explanations emphasise the importance of the interaction between far right-wing parties and other competitors. POS explanations tend to posit that institutional factors such as the electoral system (Carter 2002), the potential of the mainstream right-wing competitor to absorb right-wing voters (Ellwood 1995; Chhibber and Torcal 1997) and the fragmentation of the right (Marchi 2013) determine far right-wing party success. DOS (Koopmans and Statham 1999), on the other hand, are explanations internal to the party. The main proposition here is that far right-wing parties are themselves able to manipulate their own demand through moderating their ideology (Kitschelt and McGann 1995; Halikiopoulou et al. 2013), adopting specific rhetorical strategies, the charisma of the leader (Eatwell 2005) and party organisation and campaigning (Goodwin 2011).

DOI: 10.1057/9781137535917.0005

How may we place the rise of the Golden Dawn within this broad theoretical framework? The Golden Dawn arose in Greece at a time of severe economic crisis resulting in recession, high rates of government deficit as a percentage of GDP, high levels of unemployment, and stern austerity measures. It makes sense to seek causal links between the Eurozone crisis and the rise of the Golden Dawn. However, it would be limited to assume that people's grievances automatically translate into far right-wing party mobilisation. Other European countries that were also severely affected by the Eurozone crisis, including Portugal, Ireland, Cyprus, Spain, and Italy, did not experience a comparable rise in support for the far right. Looking to supply, the crisis in Greece also resulted in the fragmentation of the party system, allowing small parties to enter the political scene. However, it is also limited to assume that political opportunities will automatically lead to the rise of far right-wing parties. While in some of the most severely affected countries noted here the main parties were weakened, allowing for smaller parties to enter the system, it was far left-wing parties that benefitted from this. Examples include the Spanish Podemos and the Irish Sinn Feín. Taking the DOS framework into account, we could argue that the Golden Dawn has been successful because of the rhetoric it puts forward. However, the National Popular Front (*Εθνικό Λαϊκό Μέτωπο* – ELAM), the Golden Dawn's sister party in crisis-ridden Cyprus, which has adopted a similar discourse, has not enjoyed similar levels of success. Therefore, neither demand- nor supply-side explanations in themselves fully capture the dynamics of far right-wing party support. In order to understand the rise of the Golden Dawn, we need to appreciate the interaction of demand- and supply-side within the context of a crisis that was more than just economic but rather shook the foundations of the Greek nation-state and its democratic institutions.

The crisis of the Greek nation-state and the Golden Dawn's nationalist solution

This book progresses beyond the state of the art and focuses on the ways in which the Golden Dawn has capitalised on favourable demand-side conditions by offering a nationalist solution to what was seen as a crisis of the nation-state. The European sovereign debt crisis had implications in Greece that go well beyond the economic sphere. It was followed by

DOI: 10.1057/9781137535917.0005

a political crisis characterised by high levels of electoral volatility and party system fragmentation, resulting in the implosion of the party system. This reshaped long-standing dynamics of party competition and fully discredited the main political actors of the *metapolitefsi* era. This in turn resulted in a major ideological crisis: essentially what was at stake was not the party system alone, but the legitimacy of the state and its capacity to mediate the effects of the crisis and provide basic services. The economic, political and ideological dimensions of the crisis challenged the system and shook its foundations. The crisis in Greece, therefore, was more than economic. It was a crisis of the nation-state and its democratic institutions. The success of the Golden Dawn must be understood precisely within this context: as dependent on the extent to which it was able to propound plausible solutions to the three sets of crises—economic, political, and ideological—that befell Greece and culminated in an overall crisis of democracy to which the Golden Dawn offered a nationalist solution.

Nationalist doctrine provides the basis for the legitimacy of the modern nation-state. Those belonging to the same nation enter into a solidarity pact, which is guarded by the state. Nationalism is the contract that binds this social pact (Wimmer 1997). Crises tend to intensify nationalism (Brubaker 2011). They 'produce more aggressive and chiliastic assertions of the national mission and evoke more powerful images of national exclusiveness and ethnic election' (Smith 1999: 348). The nature of the Greek crisis and the fact that its economic, political and ideological dimensions challenged the Greek nation-state at its core opened a political opportunity for the Golden Dawn to present itself as the saviour of the nation and defender of the national mission. Like fascist movements of the past, the Golden Dawn puts forward 'a "palin-genetic myth" of populist ultra-nationalism, seeking a nation rising Phoenix-like from the ashes of an old decadent social order' (Mann 2004: 12; Griffin 1991).

The Golden Dawn's master narrative centres on nationalism, and more specifically on the twin fascist myths of social decadence and national rebirth (Griffin 1991; Rydgren 2007). We trace the dialectical process from degenerate social condition to the purging of impure elements in order to arrive to the ultimate goal of national purification and rebirth through Mann's (2004) analysis, which focuses on nationalism, paramilitarism, statism, transcendence, and cleansing. The Golden Dawn's ability to legitimate its statism, cleansing, and support for violence through a

DOI: 10.1057/9781137535917.0005

narrative that focuses on the need to revive and awaken the nation from its current degenerate condition is at the heart of its appeal.

We examine this national revival through the framework of ethnic election. In particular, we understand the dramatic rise of the Golden Dawn and the party's ability to legitimise fascist ideals, through Smith's (1999) framework of chosenness, ethnic election, and national destiny. This framework captures the Golden Dawn's palingenetic ultra-nationalism through a focus on four aspects of ethnic election:

1   The constant reinforcement of a strict boundary between the ethnic community and the other: the Golden Dawn cultivates a distinction between ethnic Greeks, who are racially, morally and culturally superior to other groups, and foreigners who are both inferior and corrupt. As such, its rhetoric is replete with appeals to preserve Greek national identity and its ascriptive traits, including the Greek language, which has survived from antiquity; and Greek Orthodoxy, the religion of the glorious Byzantine Empire. These traits are exclusive, organic and inherited by birth.

2   A sense of moral superiority over outsiders: the Golden Dawn portrays the Greek nation as inherently superior because of ascriptive Greek traits such as bravery, valour, heroism, and sacrifice for the nation. The distinguishing feature between 'us' and 'the other' is ethnic superiority based on an idealised vision of Greece and an element of ethnic 'chosenness'. This chosenness stems from Greece's glorious past, the civilization of the ancient Greek city-states, the legacy of Orthodox Byzantium, and its sacred linguistic ethnie.

3   A doctrine of spiritual liberation that emphasises the community's special destiny and tends to include a radical reversal from its current underdog status: the Golden Dawn portrays the Greek nation as great and as having been wronged by external powers. The primary goal is the restoration of past glory. The discourse of the Golden Dawn tends to be underpinned by a language of liberation, restoration of national sovereignty, resistance to foreign domination, and struggle against external impositions.

4   The necessity of an elite-driven mobilisation: The restoration of Greece's past glory can only be initiated by authentic nationalists, who are none other than the Golden Dawn. The party therefore has a 'calling' to save the Greek nation from exploitative foreigners

DOI: 10.1057/9781137535917.0005

and domestic traitors who have collaborated with them, and thus restore Greece to its past greatness as the helm of Western civilization. It is through this calling that the party legitimates the concept of an all-powerful leader who is presented not in elitist terms but as the embodiment of the masses.

The success of the Golden Dawn lies in its ability to justify its violence and authoritarianism through ethnic election appeals and the use of palingenetic populist ultra-nationalism, which defines 'us' as the nationalists and 'them' as the enemies of the nation at a time when the nation-state is in crisis. Appealing to those who consider themselves patriots, and have been let down by the political mainstream, Golden Dawn presents a story in which the Greek predicament is a result of those foreign exploitative powers who seek to destroy Greece and their domestic collaborators who are part of that decadent social order. The resonance of this story is what has gained Golden Dawn its diverse electoral base. Many of its supporters may not believe that it is a neo-Nazi or neo-fascist party. Instead, it is the only party that addresses the crisis in all its dimensions by propounding a solution that will salvage both nation and state. This is why, perhaps unlike the other far right-wing parties in Europe, the Golden Dawn has managed to attract voters from a broad socio-demographic range.

Methods and sources

In line with our argument, which focuses on the interaction between demand and supply, we combine quantitative analysis of voting behaviour with qualitative analysis of party documents in order to examine the rise of the Golden Dawn. First, we examine the context in which the economic crisis was translated into a political and ideological crisis with significant implications for the legitimacy of the nation and the state. For the economic effect of the crisis, we look at economic indicators, including deficit as a percentage of GDP and unemployment levels. For the political effect of the crisis, we examine Greece's standing on world governance indicators, including political stability, government effectiveness, regulatory quality, rule of law and control of corruption. Finally, we examine electoral results to capture Golden Dawn's performance over time in local, national and European Parliament elections.

DOI: 10.1057/9781137535917.0005

Second, we conduct analysis of voting behaviour. Our rationale is to identify which sectors of the population are more likely to vote for the Golden Dawn. The individual-level data are derived from the Hellenic Panel Component of the Voter Study of the European Election Study 2014 (Andreadis et al. 2014). This is an EU-wide survey conducted among representative samples of the electorates of the member states, which focuses on party choices, past voting behaviour, and propensity to support specific parties. It also includes questions on political attitudes and background socio-demographic characteristics. Post-stratification adjustments have been applied on the Hellenic component of the European Election Study (EES) dataset in order to reduce the bias of the estimates (Andreadis 2014). The quantitative study examines the party's electoral base and combines descriptive with inferential statistics. We report Golden Dawn voters' answers in terms of vote choice criteria in comparison to the EES sample in order to identify possible similarities and differences. We test the applicability of two major demand-side theories, including the socio-economic and political grievance models, on the probability of a Greek citizen to opt for the Golden Dawn. In doing so, we evaluate the explanatory power of these two models in the Greek context and identify the factors that make voting for the Golden Dawn more likely.

Third, we analyse Golden Dawn materials in order to show how the party capitalises on demand by putting forward its social decadence and nationalist palingenetic myths. We have carried out qualitative analysis of Golden Dawn online materials uploaded on the Golden Dawn website between April 2012 and September 2014 under the sections 'current affairs', 'ideological texts', 'history', and 'civilisation'. These texts amount to over 1,500 documents. We contextualise the ideological components of the social decadence and national rebirth myths in the discourse and the programmatic agenda of the Golden Dawn. We proceed to analyse the role of the nation within Golden Dawn's ideology and then place the party's mobilisation appeals within the national awakening framework.

Chapter outline

This book seeks to understand the rise of the Golden Dawn. It is structured as follows:

DOI: 10.1057/9781137535917.0005

Chapter 2 contextualises the rise of the Golden Dawn within the framework of the Greek crisis. It commences with a short overview of the Golden Dawn's electoral performance over time since its establishment in the 1980s, with an emphasis on the breakthrough the party experienced in 2012. The chapter continues with an analysis of the Greek crisis, showing that, beyond its economic dimension, its political and ideological facets culminated into a broader crisis of the nation-state. The chapter examines the ways in which this crisis altered political dynamics and offered the Golden Dawn increased opportunities. The overall rationale is to place the rise of the Golden Dawn within a favourable environment characterised by the interdependence of demand- and supply-side dynamics.

Chapter 3 evaluates demand-side explanations for the rise of the Golden Dawn through an examination of the socio-demographic profile and political attitudes of its prospective supporters. It places support for the Golden Dawn within the broader European comparative framework, which identifies two main models of far right-wing party support, that is, the socio-economic and political grievance models. The chapter finds that the keys to the Golden Dawn's support are grievance, anxiousness, bewilderment, insecurity, and resentfulness, which prompt voters to support a party that propagates return to traditional values.

Chapter 4 focuses on the ways in which the Golden Dawn has shaped its own demand through its ideology, discourse and programmatic agenda. It examines the Golden Dawn's nationalist solution to the Greek crisis within the framework of fascist political myths and more specifically the myth of social decadence. The chapter first examines fascism and the myth of social decadence from a theoretical perspective. It proceeds by contextualising the ideological components of this myth in the discourse and programmatic agenda of the Golden Dawn by breaking down the Golden Dawn's populist nation-statism—as the key answer to the social decadence problem—into the following fascist principles: popular supremacy, paramilitarism/violence, and transcendence and cleansing.

Chapter 5 focuses on the second component of the Golden Dawn's nationalist solution, namely, the fascist myth of national rebirth. The chapter places the Golden Dawn's palingenetic vision within the framework of ethnic election and examines the ways in which the party draws upon available cultural reservoirs. Its main proposition is that the Greek crisis offered fertile ground for the Golden Dawn to present itself as the

DOI: 10.1057/9781137535917.0005

saviour of the nation and defender of the national mission. We show that this type of nationalism forms the Golden Dawn's master narrative and argue that the party's success is partly related to its ability to claim ownership of nationalist issues through employing a narrative of chosenness and ethnic election.

The aim of Chapter 6 is two-fold. First, it summarises the main arguments and findings of the book, focusing on demand- and supply-side dynamics. More specifically, the chapter discusses the ways in which the Golden Dawn has capitalised on social discontent by putting forward its 'nationalist solution', that is, a discourse, which emphasises the twin fascist myths of societal decline and national rebirth. Second, the chapter places the Golden Dawn within the broader framework of democratic politics and Greek political culture, discussing the potential implications of this phenomenon on policy and the political mainstream.

DOI: 10.1057/9781137535917.0005

2
The Rise of the Golden Dawn in the Context of the Greek Crisis

Abstract: *This chapter contextualises the rise of the Golden Dawn within the framework of the Greek crisis. It commences with a short overview of the Golden Dawn's electoral performance over time since its establishment in the 1980s, with an emphasis on the breakthrough the party experienced in 2012. The chapter continues with an analysis of the Greek crisis, showing that beyond its economic dimension, its political and ideological facets culminated into a broader crisis of the nation-state. The chapter examines the ways in which this crisis altered political dynamics and offered the Golden Dawn increased opportunities. The overall rationale is to place the rise of the Golden Dawn within a favourable environment characterised by the interdependence of demand- and supply-side dynamics.*

Keywords: elections; Greek crisis; Greek political system

Vasilopoulou, Sofia and Daphne Halikiopoulou. *The Golden Dawn's 'Nationalist Solution': Explaining the Rise of the Far Right in Greece.* New York: Palgrave Macmillan, 2015. DOI: 10.1057/9781137535917.0006.

Introduction

The aim of this chapter is to contextualise the rise of the Golden Dawn within the framework of the Greek crisis. The chapter commences with a short overview of the Golden Dawn's electoral performance over time since its establishment in the 1980s, with an emphasis on the breakthrough the party experienced in 2012. Placing this within the dynamics of party competition in Greece, we show that the Greek political system of the post-dictatorship (*metapolitefsi*) era, as well as the Golden Dawn's own pariah status, served to marginalise the party. The Eurozone crisis altered these dynamics. The chapter continues with an analysis of the Greek crisis, showing that beyond its economic dimension, its political and ideological facets culminated into a broader crisis of the nation-state and its democratic institutions, facilitating the rise of the Golden Dawn. Essentially the crisis in Greece challenged the capacity of the state and questioned its ability to fulfil its social contract obligations. Not only did it change the dynamics of the Greek party system by resulting in the implosion of the two main parties, but more importantly it challenged the basis of the Greek state, questioning the legitimacy, and by extension the stability, of Greek democratic institutions. The inability of the Greek state to address the crisis became perceived as a breach of the social contract that holds the nation-state together. More than a fiscal predicament, the Greek crisis became a crisis of legitimacy, a crisis of democracy, a crisis of the nation-state. We examine the ways in which this broader crisis of the nation-state altered political dynamics and offered the Golden Dawn increased opportunities. Our overall rationale is to place the rise of the Golden Dawn within a favourable environment characterised by the interdependence of demand- and supply-side dynamics.

The Golden Dawn: from margins to success

The Golden Dawn is not a new group. It began in the form of a bulletin published in December 1980 by a group of former members of the neo-fascist 'Party of August 4th', associated with the dictatorial regime of Metaxas (1936–1941). The Golden Dawn differentiated itself ideologically from other Greek far right-wing factions, especially those related to the Colonels' junta regime (1967–1974), by emphasising its Nationalist Socialist principles (Psarras 2012: 35) and more specifically the popular

DOI: 10.1057/9781137535917.0006

basis of its authoritarianism. The group was formally established under the name 'Popular Association—Golden Dawn' in 1983 (Ellinas 2013). It remained, however, inactive until the early 1990s. This is partly because of the links between the leader of the group, Nikos Michaloliakos, and the National Political Union (*Εθνική Πολιτική Ένωση*, EPEN), formed in 1984 by the former leader of the Greek Colonels' regime, Georgios Papadopoulos. In 1984 Michaloliakos became the president of EPEN's youth. However, there was a fundamental ideological schism between the Nationalist Socialist principles of the Golden Dawn leader and the military right-wing principles of the Greek Junta regime (Hasapopoulos 2013). It was this schism and personality clashes that led to Michaloliakos's resignation from EPEN and the reinstatement of the bulletin in the late 1980s. In 1993 Golden Dawn assumed a 'movement' role. The first time it officially ran for elections was in 1994, although its political presence was overall irregular in the 1990s and 2000s. Its political participation was essentially halted between 1996 and 2009, partly linked to the party's violent activities, indictment of its members and blatant associations with Nazi ideology.

Since its establishment in the 1980s the Golden Dawn has been notorious for perpetrating violent and hate acts. Political violence in the 1980s, 1990s and 2000s was perpetrated against left-wing school and university students, members of Marxist organisations and trade unions. One example is the notorious case of 'Periandros', formally known as Antonis Androutsopoulos, the second in command of the Golden Dawn who was accused and subsequently imprisoned for the attempted murder of left-wing student Dimitris Kousouris in 1998. Violence was also directed against immigrants of various ethnicities, including those of Turkish, Kurdish, African and Albanian origins. Also targeted were those members of pro-immigration and anti-racism organisations. The party confined itself to extra-parliamentary activities that tended to involve violence at the street-level, while it remained in the margins of the Greek political system enjoying very little electoral success.

The first time the Golden Dawn elected a representative was during the 2010 local and municipal elections when the party leader Nikos Michaloliakos became a local councillor with 5.29 per cent of the votes. The party's real electoral breakthrough came in May 2012 when the party received 6.97 per cent. Defying the urban-rural divide, the party performed well in both urban and peripheral constituencies. In the capital Athens, it received 8.77 (A Athinon) and 6.71 per cent (B Athinon).

DOI: 10.1057/9781137535917.0006

Similarly in the centre and the periphery of Piraeus, the party received 8.88 and 9.49 per cent, respectively. In the constituency of Attica, Golden Dawn gained 9.7 per cent. It also performed well in Greece's second largest city, Thessaloniki, with 6.91 per cent in central Thessaloniki (A Thessaloniki) and 7.85 per cent in Thessaloniki's periphery (B Thessaloniki). These levels of support were consistent in semi-urban centres, including Achaia with 6.32 per cent, Aetoloakarnania with 7.92 per cent, Ileia with 7.85 per cent, and the Dodekanese with 6.13 per cent. Among the highest results were recorded in Corinth with 11.99 per cent and Lakonia with 10.19 per cent.

In the subsequent June 2012 election, the party's performance was similar, characterised by a marginal decline at 0.05 per cent. The party received 6.92 per cent compared to May's 6.97 per cent. The party experienced low levels of electoral volatility, with 84.2 per cent of its 6 May voters remaining loyal to it in June (VPRC 2012). It retained its support in many constituencies across Greece, again defying the urban-rural divide. In fact among the highest results were observed in some peripheral areas including a 10.7 per cent in Lakonia and 9.9 per cent in Corinth, as well as urban centres including 8.8 per cent in central Athens (A Athinon) and 9.5 per cent in Piraeus periphery (B Pireos). The party even received support in the constituencies of Distomo (6.4 per cent) and Kalavryta (6.2 per cent), which are known in Greece as historical areas that suffered Nazi atrocities during the Second World War. This result came contrary to assessments that the Golden Dawn would decline, especially after an incident of violence perpetrated on behalf of a Golden Dawn MP against a representative of the Communist Party of Greece (*Κομμουνιστικό Κόμμα Ελλάδας*, KKE) on national television. The Golden Dawn vote was mostly interpreted as a protest vote, cast by an angry electorate that refuses to pay the price of austerity. The overwhelming reasons quoted behind voting intention for this party were protest, indignation and punishment (29 per cent), followed by the immigration issue (27 per cent), agreement with its policies (14 per cent), and patriotism (13 per cent) (Public Issue 2012).

Table 2.1 shows its electoral results in national and European Parliamentary elections when the party stood alone. During the 1990s and 2000s, the Golden Dawn also participated in the electoral competition as part of various far right-wing alliances but with limited success.

The Golden Dawn retained its support during the 2014 European Parliament and local elections despite the fact that the violent incidents

DOI: 10.1057/9781137535917.0006

TABLE 2.1   *Golden Dawn election results since 1994 (national and European)*

Year	Election	Percentage	Votes	Seats
1994	European	0.11	7,242	0
1996	Parliamentary	0.07	4,487	0
2009	European	0.46	23,609	0
2009	Parliamentary	0.29	19,624	0
2012 May	Parliamentary	6.97	440,966	21
2012 June	Parliamentary	6.92	426,025	18
2014	European	9.39	536,910	3

Source: Greek Ministry of the Interior (www.ypes.gr). Note that in other years the Golden Dawn has run as part of an alliance with various far right-wing organisations. These have not been included in this table.

continued and intensified in nature. Violence against immigrants and Greeks of opposing political persuasions, notably the murder of left-wing activist Pavlos Fyssas in 2013, culminated in a series of arrests and the subsequent imprisonment of its leader and MPs. However, pending indictment, the party was allowed to run for elections in 2014. Despite prognoses that this would lead to a significant decline in its support, the party widened and strengthened its electoral base coming third after the Coalition of the Radical Left (*Συνασπισμός Ριζοσπαστικής Αριστεράς*, SYRIZA) and the centre-right New Democracy (*Νέα Δημοκρατία*, ND) and gaining three European Parliament seats with 9.39 per cent of the Greek vote. In the 2014 local and municipal elections,[1] the party gained seats across Greece. Notably in the municipality of Attica the party gained six seats, three in Central Macedonia and two in Eastern Macedonia and Thrace, Western Greece, Epirus, Thessaly, Southern Aegean, the Peloponnese and Mainland Greece, respectively. In terms of local councils, the party gained four seats in Athens, two in Thessaloniki and one in Piraeus (see Tables 2.2 and 2.3). While on the one hand, European Parliament and local elections are generally regarded as 'second order' elections (Reif and Schmitt 1980), entailing that there is a higher likelihood of protest, on the other hand, the implication of this result for national politics is significant especially when the results confirm the national trend.

What explains the sudden rise of such a previously marginalised group with clear links to Nazi ideological principles and notoriety of association with violence?

DOI: 10.1057/9781137535917.0006

TABLE 2.2   *Municipal election results, 2014*

Municipalities	Seats
Eastern Macedonia and Thrace	2
Attica	6
Northern Aegean	0
Western Greece	2
Western Macedonia	1
Epirus	2
Thessaly	2
Ionian islands	1
Central Macedonia	3
Crete	1
Southern Aegean	2
Peloponnese	2
Mainland Greece	2

Source: Greek Ministry of the Interior (www.ypes.gr).

TABLE 2.3   *Local election results, 2014*

Local councils	Seats
Athens (centre)	4
Thessaloniki	2
Patra	0
Heraklion	0
Piraeus	1
Larissa	0
Volos	0
Peristeri	0
Rhodes	0
Ioannina	0

Note: that only major local councils are included.

Source: Greek Ministry of the Interior (www.ypes.gr).

The political context

The far right in Greece has been mostly confined to the margins of the party system since the collapse of the junta regime and the subsequent restoration of democracy in 1974. Various far right-wing parties includ-ing the National Democratic Union (*Εθνική Δημοκρατική Ένωση*), the National Alignment (*Εθνική Παράταξις*), the Progressive Party (*Κόμμα Προοδευτικών*), the National Political Union (*Εθνική Πολιτική Ένωση*),

DOI: 10.1057/9781137535917.0006

the Hellenic Front (*Ελληνικό Μέτωπο*) and the Front Line (*Πρώτη Γραμμή*) have at times competed in national, local and European elections but with limited and short-lived success. During the 1977 Greek parliament elections the National Alignment received 6.8 per cent of the vote, translating into five seats out of three hundred. During the 1981 European elections, the Progressive Party received 2 per cent of the vote, translating into one European Parliament (EP) seat. In 1984, the National Political Union received 2.3 per cent of the vote, gaining one EP seat. The first far right-wing party to experience parliamentary representation since 1984 is the Popular Orthodox Rally (*Λαϊκός Ορθόδοξος Συναγερμός*, LAOS), a faction of New Democracy which entered the European Parliament in 2004 receiving 4.12 per cent of the vote and one seat; the national parliament in 2007 with 3.8 per cent of the vote and ten seats; and the national parliament in 2009 with 5.6 per cent of the vote and fifteen seats.

Political opportunity structures (POS) dynamics provide a partial explanation for this. First, the fragmentation of the right into various movements unwilling to coalesce rendered these groups weak electoral contenders that were often competing against each other. Second, the association of far right groups with the Colonels' Junta regime rendered them illegitimate in the eyes of the Greek voters. It could be argued that the centre-right New Democracy was able to attract votes from those Greek voters with ultra-nationalist, pro-monarchist and generally far right-wing views while offering a more legitimate option (Georgiadou 2011). Third, the Greek party system of the metapolitefsi era has not been conducive to far right-wing parties. Greece's electoral system, a form of reinforced proportional representation, and the bipolar nature of its party system, favours large parties. Since 1974 the Greek party system has been dominated by two main parties, the centre-left Panhellenic Socialist Movement (*Πανελλήνιο Σοσιαλιστικό Κίνημα*, PASOK) and the centre-right New Democracy. Elections have consistently produced single-party majority governments with few exceptions. Coalitions have been rare and short-lived. Greece had a 'national unity' government from July to November 1974, which was responsible for organising the first post-junta parliamentary elections; a coalition government between New Democracy and the Coalition of the Left and Progress (*Συνασπισμός της Αριστεράς και της προόδου*, SYNASPISMOS),[2] which lasted approximately five months (from June to October 1989) and ended following New Democracy's withdrawal; and an 'ecumenical' government

DOI: 10.1057/9781137535917.0006

comprising of New Democracy, PASOK and SYNASPISMOS, which lasted under a year (from November 1989 until April 1990) (Lyrintzis and Nikolakopoulos 2004: 99). Apart from these exceptions and given that third parties cannot prevent any of the two major centre-left and centre-right parties from forming a majority government, Pappas (2003) concludes that Greece is a classic two-party system. Greece has had an effective number of parties at the legislative level between 2.1 and 2.4 (Pappas 2003: 102; Gallagher et al. 2006: 364). From 1977 until the last pre-crisis elections in 2009 PASOK and New Democracy have jointly gained between a minimum of 251 (in 2009) and a maximum of 287 (in 1981 and 1985) seats (see Table 2.4). In six elections their combined electoral gains surpassed 85 per cent.

The Greek political system, therefore, marginalised the Golden Dawn. The dynamics of party competition, as well as the de-legitimisation of right-wing extremism after the collapse of the junta, the fragmentation of the right into various far right-wing factions, the ability of New Democracy to absorb right-wing voters of all convictions, as well as the Golden Dawn's own association with violence, prevented the party from entering the political scene. The Eurozone crisis, however, altered political dynamics. Not only did it change the dynamics of the Greek party system and party competition, opening up political opportunities for parties on the fringes; by translating into a political and ideological

TABLE 2.4   *PASOK and New Democracy election results and seats, 1977–2009*

Election year	PASOK		New Democracy		Total combined	
	Percentage	Seats	Percentage	Seats	Percentage	Seats
1977	25.3	93	41.8	171	67.1	264
1981	48.1	172	35.9	115	84	287
1985	45.8	161	40.8	126	86.6	287
1989 June	39.1	125	44.3	145	83.4	270
1989 Nov	40.7	128	46.2	148	86.9	276
1990	38.6	123	46.9	150	85.5	273
1993	46.9	170	39.3	111	86.2	281
1996	41.5	162	38.1	108	79.6	270
2000	43.8	158	42.7	125	86.5	283
2004	40.5	117	45.4	165	85.9	282
2007	38.1	102	41.8	152	79.9	254
2009	43.9	160	33.5	91	77.3	251

Source: Greek Parliament website at: http://www.hellenicparliament.gr/
Vouli-ton-Ellinon/To-Politevma/Ekloges/Eklogika-apotelesmata-New/#B.

DOI: 10.1057/9781137535917.0006

crisis, it shook the foundations of the Greek nation-state challenging the basis of Greek democratic institutions and the legitimacy of the regime itself.

The Greek crisis

With the eruption of the Eurozone crisis, Greece plunged into deep recession, threatening to destabilise the whole euro area. PASOK's 2009 government, despite its ambitious pre-electoral promise of a €3 billion stimulus package, instead sought a package of financial aid from the European Union (EU) and the International Monetary Fund (IMF) on 23 April 2010 (Gemenis 2010: 361). The rescue package amounting to €110 billion led to the adoption of a number of highly controversial reforms, stringent austerity measures and a wave of trade union protests and strikes. In 2011 the crisis deepened. The government put forward its €28 billion Medium Term Fiscal Strategy 2012–2015 Plan, which was approved by Greek lawmakers (155 in favour out of a total of 300 MPs) on 28 June 2011 amidst intense popular discontent and violent clashes between protesters and the Greek police (*Ta Nea* 2011). During this period, credit rating agencies downgraded Greece's rating, warning for the possibility of the country's default. In an EU Summit held on 26–27 October 2011 Greece's European partners agreed a 50 per cent bond debt 'haircut' known as the private sector involvement (PSI) in return for additional austerity measures.[3]

On 31 October, then prime minister George A. Papandreou announced a controversial plan to hold a referendum over the bilateral loan agreement between Greece and its lenders that was negotiated at the time (*To Vima* 2011). The rationale behind this announcement was to turn the referendum into a vote of confidence for his government, gain a clear popular mandate for the adoption of further austerity measures and avoid the prospect of early elections. This initiative backfired, as it did not receive the support of Greece's European partners. Only a few days later on 9 November Papandreou announced his resignation and on 11 November a government of national unity between PASOK, New Democracy and LAOS was formed under the leadership of Lucas Papademos, a former head of the Bank of Greece. In February 2012 the interim coalition government approved a new package of unpopular austerity measures in return for a €130 billion bailout fund. On 11 April,

DOI: 10.1057/9781137535917.0006

a date that coincided with Holy Wednesday of the Greek Orthodox Easter, 6 May was set as the legislative election date. By that day, Greece had signed two Memorandums of Understanding setting the economic policy conditionality between Greece and its lenders, one in May 2010 and a second in early 2012.

Austerity measures increased taxation, targeting income tax, VAT and property taxes. VAT rose from 19 per cent to 23 per cent. The tax-free threshold for income was lowered significantly. Many sectors of the population suffered, especially the middle class. Homeowners were targeted to pay large sums in the form of property tax, and many were unable to do so losing their homes. Salaries, especially public sector salaries and pensions, were significantly reduced, with some reductions as high as 40 or 50 per cent. The Greek government abolished the two extra monthly salaries per annum, known as the '13th and 14th' salaries, which was seen as a controversial measure. Public investment was cut and subsidies for local government were reduced. Welfare spending, including education, health, and benefits, were also targeted. This was accompanied by increasing levels of unemployment. The rise of total unemployment between 2009 and 2013 is stark, increasing from 9.6 per cent in 2009 to 17.9 per cent in 2011 and 27.5 per cent in 2013. Youth unemployment (those under 25) rose from 25.7 per cent in 2009 to 44.7 per cent in 2011 and 58.3 per cent in 2013 (Eurostat 2014).

Greece's economic deficiencies, including its inability to refinance its high public debt and manage its worsening deficit, culminated to a political crisis. The May and June 2012 elections were characterised by high levels of electoral volatility and the fragmentation of the party system. The 6 May electoral results shook the main pillars of the Greek political system, engendering the breakdown of the two-party domination of the political scene. PASOK and New Democracy jointly gained merely 32 per cent of the vote. This translated into 41 and 108 parliamentary seats respectively, which did not allow either party to form a majority government. Anti-bailout, anti-establishment and populist forces made substantial gains including SYRIZA with 16.8 per cent, Independent Greeks (*Ανεξάρτητοι Έλληνες*, ANEL), a splinter party from New Democracy formed in February 2012, with 10.6 per cent and the Golden Dawn with 6.97 per cent of the votes cast.

The June 2012 electoral results maintained many of the trends established in the previous round, including the fragmentation of the two-party system, the electoral decline of PASOK and the rise of anti-establishment

DOI: 10.1057/9781137535917.0006

parties. Both New Democracy and SYRIZA witnessed a country-wide rise, across most constituencies in the country, and gained voters from across the spectrum compared to 6 May. New Democracy received 29.7 per cent of the vote and SYRIZA came second with 26.9 per cent. By contrast, most other parties lost support nation-wide, except the Democratic Left (*Δημοκρατική Αριστερά*, DIMAR) which gained 0.15 per cent. PASOK received a mere 12.3 per cent; ANEL 7.5 per cent and KKE 4.5 per cent. The Golden Dawn lost marginally, receiving 6.92 per cent. The June election entrenched the new societal division between those who supported and those who opposed the terms of the two bailout agreements Greece had signed with its lenders. Despite different specific stipulations, both memoranda had become associated with severe austerity measures and these came to represent the pro- and anti-bailout camps. This division transcends left-right politics, as parties of both the left and the right opposed the bailout. The larger parties that were in favour—and indeed part of the political establishment—supported the bailout package, whereas the smaller anti-establishment parties espousing radical ideologies were against it. The pro-bailout camp included the mainstream New Democracy and PASOK, while the anti-bailout camp consisted of the fringe (radical or extreme) SYRIZA, KKE, DIMAR, ANEL, and Golden Dawn (see Table 2.5).

TABLE 2.5   *Greek national election results, May and June 2012 (turnout in brackets)*

	6 May 2012 (65.12%)			17 June 2012 (62.49%)		
	Seats		Votes	Seats		Votes
Parties	N	%	(%)	N	%	(%)
NEW DEMOCRACY	108	36	18.8	129	43	29.7
SYRIZA	52	17.3	16.8	71	23.67	26.9
PASOK	41	13.7	13.2	33	11	12.3
ANEL	33	11	10.6	20	6.67	7.5
GOLDEN DAWN	21	7	7	18	6	6.9
DIMAR	19	6.3	6.1	17	5.67	6.3
KKE	26	8.7	8.5	12	4	4.5
ECO-GREENS	0	0	2.9	0	0	0.9
LAOS	0	0	2.9	0	0	1.6
DEMOCRATIC ALLIANCE	0	0	2.5	–	–	–
RECREATE GREECE!	0	0	2.1	0	0	1.6
DRASI	0	0	1.8	–	–	–
OTHER	0	0	6.7	0	0	1.9

Source: Greek Ministry of the Interior (www.ypes.gr).

DOI: 10.1057/9781137535917.0006

The political dimension of the crisis significantly altered the dynamics of party competition, opening political opportunities for parties of the fringe belonging to the anti-bailout camp. The implosion of LAOS, the loss of its anti-systemic status and its association with the austerity measures opened further opportunities for parties of the right (Ellinas 2013). The implications of the crisis, however, were deeper than that, as the economic and political instability also had a fundamental systemic dimension: they revealed the weaknesses of Greek democratic institutions and the inability of the state to mediate any crisis.

The Greek sovereign debt crisis occurred against the backdrop of embedded clientelism and corruption. The *metapolitefsi* system operated within a framework of consolidated mass clientelism that transcends left-right divisions—what Mouzelis and Pagoulatos (2002) term 'partitocratic' democracy. Featherstone (2005) has characterised Greece as a *'société bloquée'*, that is, a society where systemic weaknesses including historically embedded clientelism, rent-seeking behaviour, the near absence of policy communities and think-tanks, and a regime of 'disjointed corporatism' create problems with regard to the country's governability impeding any reform attempts. Large-scale deeply embedded corruption has entailed a lack of accountability as essentially separate agents govern the entire system. These rent-seeking groups have vested interests in curtailing competition, increasing bureaucracy and hindering transparency in order to maximise their gains (Mitsopoulos and Pelagidis 2011). The two main parties have relied heavily on and perpetuated this rent-seeking behaviour, using their privileged access to the state as a means of providing rents in exchange for votes. This consolidated clientelism weakened Greek democratic institutions and significantly impeded upon the state's capacity for reform and the provision of public services during an impending crisis.

Therefore the economic and political crises culminated into a crisis of nation, state and democracy. This is because they revealed the extent to which the Greek state was in a poor position to address an impending crisis. An examination of good governance indicators since 2003 confirms that Greek citizens' perception of governance effectiveness has been in steady decline.

Figure 2.1 shows how Greece fares in the following five good governance indicators (Kaufmann et al. 2010):

DOI: 10.1057/9781137535917.0006

Indicator	Country	Year	Percentile rank (0 to 100)
Political stability and absence of violence/terrorism	Greece	2003	
		2008	
		2013	
Government effectiveness	Greece	2003	
		2008	
		2013	
Regulatory quality	Greece	2003	
		2008	
		2013	
Rule of law	Greece	2003	
		2008	
		2013	
Control of corruption	Greece	2003	
		2008	
		2013	

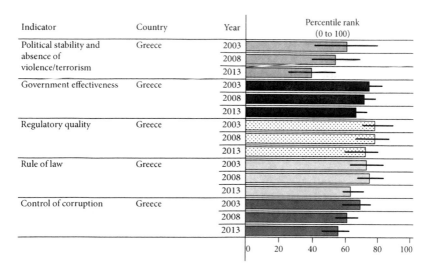

FIGURE 2.1   *Worldwide governance indicators, Greece*
Source: http://info.worldbank.org/governance/wgi/index.aspx#reports.

▶ Political Stability and Absence of Violence/Terrorism, which captures perceptions of government stability and its susceptibility to be removed by violent means.

▶ Government Effectiveness, which refers to citizens' perceptions of the quality of public services and the credibility of the government's commitment to the implementation of such policies.

▶ Regulatory Quality, which denotes citizens' perceptions of the ability of the government to put forward policies related to private sector development.

▶ Rule of Law, which refers to citizens' perceptions regarding the impartiality and effectiveness of the justice system and its enforcement.

▶ Control of Corruption, which measures citizens' perceptions of the extent to which the state functions independently of private interests.

As Figure 2.1 indicates, between 2003 and 2013 Greece experienced a decline in all five indicators. Greek citizens' trust in the system dramatically declined within that decade. Perceptions of government stability dropped from 61.5 per cent in 2003 to 39.3 per cent in 2013. Perceptions of

DOI: 10.1057/9781137535917.0006

government effectiveness declined from 75.1 to 67 per cent. Perceptions of the ability of the government to put forward policies related to private sector development decreased from 78.9 to 72.7 per cent. People's belief in the impartiality and effectiveness of the justice system fell from 73.7 to 63.5 per cent. Finally, perceptions of the ability of the state to control corruption and function independently of private interests dropped from 69.3 to 55.5 per cent. These figures are significant not only because they show a declining trend within Greece over time, but they also show how the country fares on a global scale. In terms of political stability, Greece ranks in the 25–50th percentile range; whereas in all the other four indicators it ranks on the 50–75th percentile range. Greece scores the lowest of the other European countries that have faced similar economic crisis conditions, including Spain, Portugal and Ireland.

In other words, as the crisis progressed, Greek citizens increasingly lost their trust in the system and progressively perceived the state as ineffective. They saw the government as highly unstable; its effectiveness to provide public services limited; its ability to regulate the private sector constrained; the justice system unable to enforce law and order; and the state as partial and controlled by private interests. The role of the state is key here. If we understand the state as part of a social contract, the delivery of its collective goods, that is, services and re-distribution, are a key part of this contract (Wimmer 1997). What happened to the Greek economy had significant implications for the strength of Greece's democratic institutions and its state capacity (Pappas 2013, 2014; Pappas and O'Malley 2014). As the state became increasingly perceived as unable to limit the socio-economic impact of the crisis on individual citizens, the legitimacy of the system declined. The sovereign debt crisis exposed the state's inability to deliver on the social contract, thus undermining the legitimacy of the system. What was discredited was not only the ability of the government to formulate sound economic policy, or the ability of a particular political party to put forward a better policy agenda. Rather the very premise of the system of the *metapolitefsi* era was shown as ineffective and illegitimate. The crisis became perceived as a breach of the social contract that holds the nation-state together.

The Golden Dawn's nationalist solution appeared a viable alternative at a time when Greece faced economic, political and ideological crises. To this the party's organisational activities at the local level played a key role (Ellinas 2015 forthcoming). Offering goods and services to Greeks not only helped the party to become 'identified as an organisation that protects the residents while eliminating the foreigners' (Dinas et al. 2015 forthcoming: 10), but also most importantly to become identified as an alternative provider of the collective goods of the state, which the latter is unable to deliver. In other words, the Golden Dawn presented itself as a substitute for the state and saviour of the nation when the nation-state was in crisis. The organisation of numerous welfare provision activities such as blood donations and 'soup kitchens' intended only for Greeks, a status to be confirmed by the presentation of a Greek identity card to one of the Golden Dawn members on site, illustrates this point as does its attempt to provide an alterative health care provision again only for Greeks. In its website the Golden Dawn makes clear in bold letters that unlike the state, it is the only political institution that can and will deliver on the provisions of the social contract (Golden Dawn 05/12/2012).

Conclusion

In this chapter, we focused on the progression of the Golden Dawn from a marginal grass-roots violent street movement to a fully fledged party with parliamentary representation. In trying to understand the constraints placed on the Golden Dawn and other similar parties during the 1980s, 1990s and 2000s, we showed that the far right has been marginalised in Greece both because of the legacy of authoritarianism and the party competition dynamics of the metapolitesfi era.

On the one hand, the rise of the Golden Dawn may be understood as an oddity, a surprising phenomenon in a country that has experienced Nazi atrocities and a subsequent military dictatorship. On the other hand, the emphasis scholars place on the role societal crises play in the rise of far right-wing parties and movements points to the relevance the Greek crisis has had on the dramatic rise of the Golden Dawn since 2012. In order to capture the favourable context within which this party marked its electoral breakthrough, we have examined the sovereign debt crisis and attempted to show that its implications affected Greek society well beyond the economic sphere. The economic crisis became translated into a political crisis and resulted in the implosion of the two-party system, allowing small parties to enter the political scene. It served to weaken LAOS, which constituted a less extreme and non-violent competitor on the right. It also altered existing cleavages by adding a pro- versus anti-bailout dimension (Vasilopoulou and Halikiopoulou 2013). The political

DOI: 10.1057/9781137535917.0006

aspect of the crisis, therefore, opened up political opportunities for parties of the fringe, such as the Golden Dawn, with a protest outlook to enter the political system.

However, the crisis was more than political. By exposing the levels of corruption in Greece and revealing fundamental problems of governance, it offered anti-systemic parties the opportunity to present themselves as different from the established corrupt regime. It challenged the capacity of the state to fulfil its social contract obligations, thus triggering an ideological crisis and questioning the very basis of the legitimacy of the system. Greece differs from other countries that faced similar economic malaise, such as Portugal, Ireland and Spain, in that its state capacity was challenged. When state capacity is limited or perceived to be limited, as was the case in Greece, then the result is the de-legitimisation of the system as a whole and its ideological foundations. This is because the system becomes perceived as incapable of addressing the crisis and mediating its socio-economic effects, thus is in breach of the social contract. In other words, the crisis in Greece differed from the economic crisis that other Western European countries faced, not in terms of degree, but in terms of kind. It was a crisis of legitimacy, a crisis of democracy, a crisis of the nation-state.

It is within this context that this book will proceed to examine the Golden Dawn. The party propounded a 'nationalist solution' to a crisis that confronted nation and state and the contract that binds them together. We seek to explain the Golden Dawn by understanding the Golden Dawn—its electoral base, its motivations, its ideology, and the context within which it came to mark its electoral breakthrough. The following chapter will focus specifically on the party's electoral base. Our aim is to examine in depth the socio-economic, demographic and attitudinal characterises of those that are likely to vote for the Golden Dawn. We will then proceed to analyse the party itself and its 'nationalist solution.'

Notes

1   The party ran under the name 'Greek Dawn'.
2   The SYNASPISMOS at this stage consisted of KKE and EAR (Ελληνική Αριστερά, Greek Left) (Bitsika 2010).
3   For the press release of the Greek Ministry of Finance, see: http://www. minfin.gr/portal/en/ resource/contentObject/id/7ad6442f-1777–4d02–80fb-91191c606664.

DOI: 10.1057/9781137535917.0006

3
Who Supports the Golden Dawn? An Analysis of the Disillusioned Voter

Abstract: *This chapter evaluates demand-side explanations for the rise of the Golden Dawn through an examination of the socio-demographic profile and political attitudes of its prospective supporters. It places support for the Golden Dawn within the broader European comparative framework, which identifies two main models of far right-wing party support, that is, the socio-economic and political grievance models. The chapter finds that the key to Golden Dawn support is grievance, anxiousness, bewilderment, insecurity and resentfulness, which prompt voters to support a party that propagates return to traditional values.*

Keywords: political grievance model; socio-economic grievance model; voting behaviour

Vasilopoulou, Sofia and Daphne Halikiopoulou. *The Golden Dawn's 'Nationalist Solution': Explaining the Rise of the Far Right in Greece.* New York: Palgrave Macmillan, 2015. DOI: 10.1057/9781137535917.0007.

Introduction

The main aim of this chapter is to evaluate demand-side explanations for the rise of the Golden Dawn through an examination of the socio-demographic profile and political attitudes of its prospective supporters. The Golden Dawn is the only far right-wing party since the post-dictatorship era that has witnessed such a dramatic rise in Greece. The Greek 2012 national elections were characterised by voter de-alignment and disillusionment with mainstream parties, which resulted in the fragmentation of the party system and the rise of small anti-establishment parties of both the right and the left. In this context of high levels of electoral volatility the Golden Dawn entered the Greek national parliament with eighteen seats out of a total of three hundred. This trend was maintained in the 2014 European Parliament elections when the Golden Dawn came third in the polls with 9.4 per cent of the Greek votes. This was a great success for a party that not only is violent and racist, but also whose leader and a number of its MPs were in prison at the time, pending trial for various charges including running a criminal organisation, murder, and grievous bodily harm. This success counters a general European trend where the most successful far right-wing parties tend to be those that have managed to distance themselves from fascism. The extremist character of the Golden Dawn, its neo-Nazi principles, racism and ultra-nationalism, as well as its violence, render the party a least likely case of success especially in a country like Greece where right-wing extremism is associated with inter-war Nazi atrocities and dictatorship.

This chapter places support for the Greek Golden Dawn within the broader European comparative framework, which identifies two main models of far right-wing party support, that is, the socio-economic and political grievance models. It examines the potential explanatory value of a number of individual-level variables in terms of probability to vote for the Golden Dawn. These include socio-economic and demographic characteristics, such as gender, age, education, place of residence, income and occupation; and a number of attitudinal variables including dissatisfaction with democracy, government approval, position on European integration, left-right placement and subjective evaluation of economic condition. The analysis of the Greek voters' likelihood to opt for the Golden Dawn suggests that support for the Golden Dawn cannot be neatly associated with specific socio-economic groups in Greek society. In other words, Golden Dawn support does not necessarily 'fit'

DOI: 10.1057/9781137535917.0007

within the European-wide socio-economic grievance model. On the other hand, protest, disillusionment and dissatisfaction with both the government and the system as a whole are better predictors for Golden Dawn support. Essentially, right-wing dissatisfied anti-EU voters are more likely to vote for this party.

Our empirical analysis proceeds in two stages. We first examine the overlap in propensity to vote between the Golden Dawn and other Greek parties. We do so in order to investigate the intersection of the electorates and examine whether this is greater among parties with greater ideological proximity. We proceed by testing the applicability of the socio-economic and political grievance models on the probability of a Greek citizen to opt for the Golden Dawn. In doing so, we evaluate the explanatory power of these two models in the Greek context of 2014 and identify the factors that make voting for the Golden Dawn more likely. We report Golden Dawn voters' answers in terms of vote choice criteria for the 2014 elections in comparison to the EES sample in order to identify the extent to which protest plays a different role in vote choice among Golden Dawn supporters compared to the rest of the respondents.

The far right and its voters: a theoretical perspective

Interest in the rise of the far right was revived in the 1980s, drawing upon and developing work carried out in the 1950s and 1960s to explain the rise of inter-war fascism (e.g., Betz 1993, 1994; Kitschelt with McGann 1995; Eatwell 2000; Minkenberg 2000; Lubbers et al. 2002; Norris 2005; Van der Brug and Fennema 2007; Rydgren 2008, 2013; Lucassen and Lubbers 2011). Theories that focus on the voters themselves, their social base and their attitudinal characteristics are identified as demand-side or bottom up. These sets of theories may be broadly categorised in terms of socio-economic and attitudinal explanations. The former are based on socio-economic grievances, 'focusing on the objective—mostly macrostructurally shaped conditions that have increased grievances and discontent among the people' (Rydgren 2007: 247). The latter are based on grievances related to the functioning of democracy (Van der Brug et al. 2013). They focus on political attitudes and an overall disillusionment with politics.

The socio-economic grievance model examines the role of socio-economic grievances among certain groups of voters (Lipset 1960; Bell

DOI: 10.1057/9781137535917.0007

1964; Betz 1994; Kriesi et al. 2006, 2008). 'Support for far right-wing parties is explained by "structurally determined pathologies", which are triggered by "extreme conditions" (i.e. crises)' (Mudde 2010: 1171). This model posits that the wider process of modernisation, globalisation and de-nationalisation in Europe have brought about structural changes to European democracies. Increasing economic and cultural competition for scarce resources have created a society of 'winners' and 'losers'. The likely losers are those unable to compete in the new socio-economic space. Their preferences are unlikely to be aligned with existing parties, which represent traditional interests and 'generally tend to formulate a winners' programme' (Kriesi et al. 2006: 926). In other words, far right-wing party support may be understood as a 'psychological strain associated with uncertainties produced by large-scale socioeconomic and sociocultural changes' (Betz 1998: 8). People cast a vote for far right-wing parties as a reaction to these structural changes. Voters for the far right are 'the losers of modernity' (Betz 1994) who perceive both cultural and material threats from these structural changes to European democracies.

Objective characteristics, including income, occupation sector, employment status, gender, place of residence and education, are predictors of far right-wing party support. Male, lower educated, younger, low income, voters and those who compete with immigrants for jobs, including non-skilled and manual workers, those in part-time jobs and the unemployed form the social base of far right-wing party support (Lubbers et al. 2002). Male voters exhibit higher propensity to support far right-wing parties than female voters (Betz 1994). This difference may be due to a variety of reasons. First, authoritarianism tends to be associated with anti-feminist attitudes (Kitschelt with McGann 1995): far right-wing parties stress the importance of family values and argue that women's role is to provide the nation with native-borne children (Rippeyoung 2007). Second, women may not be attracted to far right-wing parties because of their violent nature and their association with violent activities (Mayer 1999). Third, the structure of women's participation in the workforce is different to their male counterparts. Women tend to be over-represented in non-manual jobs and the service sector. They are less likely to be blue-collar workers and as such less likely to suffer from the decline of industrialisation (Givens 2004).

Turning to employment and social class, the 'losers' of the modernisation process tend to include the unemployed and unskilled workers:

DOI: 10.1057/9781137535917.0007

blue-collar workers employed in the secondary employment sector, which includes jobs in industry, mining construction, manufacturing. Increasing international competition and the accelerated shift from secondary to tertiary sector have particularly hit unskilled, low-skilled, manual workers. These people are more likely to become unemployed and to perceive a competitive threat from immigration either related to employment or welfare redistribution (Lubbers and Scheepers 2002; Kitschelt and McGann 1995). They 'represent a readily identifiable underclass of the permanently unemployed, underemployed, or marginally employed who are quickly turning into the losers of the accelerated modernization process' (Betz 1993: 420). On the other hand given that the tertiary/service sector is the fastest growing in Europe, people employed in this sector are less likely to feel threatened. Overall, low income groups tend to be more vulnerable to changes in levels of unemployment at times of crisis. A broader analysis of class points also to the old middle classes (Lipset 1960), small entrepreneurs, self-employed and small shopkeepers threatened by large-scale industry.

In terms of education, people with the lowest education are more likely to vote for the far right (Lubbers and Scheepers 2002; Mayer 2013). Lower-educated people hold a more unfavourable attitude towards immigrants and tend to have ethno-centric authoritarian attitudes. In terms of age, the picture is ambiguous and tends to be country specific. On the one hand, older voters are more likely to have authoritarian attitudes, but on the other, they are less likely to be involved in violent activities. As a result scholars find younger males as more likely to opt for certain far right-wing parties. For example, people aged between 18 and 26 have been identified as more likely to vote for the Front National (Lubbers and Scheepers 2002). In other cases, however, older males have been identified as the voting base of parties such as the BNP and UKIP (Ford and Goodwin 2010). In terms of area of residence, studies have found that large cities with diverse populations that tend to attract large numbers of immigrants tend to exhibit lower levels of support for far right-wing parties. On the contrary, industrial cities and/or towns that have traditionally been working class strongholds tend to attract higher levels of support for the far right (Ford and Goodwin 2010). Also small towns with low immigration levels but neighbouring large multi-cultural cities are also more likely to exhibit higher levels of far right-wing party support.

DOI: 10.1057/9781137535917.0007

The political grievance model focuses on political attitudes and suggests that political disillusionment, cynicism and dissatisfaction with the system not necessarily linked to actual social status or objective economic conditions are predictors for far right-wing party support. Support for the far right is understood as the by-product of resentment, alienation and lack of trust with the political system as a whole. Far right-wing voters are those with an intention to protest, that is, voters that express dissatisfaction with the way democracy works, those who disapprove government policies and those who express Eurosceptic attitudes. While the socio-economic grievance model focuses on grievances related to objective criteria, this model focuses on grievances related to subjective criteria. This model derives from the partisan de-alignment approach, which emphasises the declining significance of cleavages as voting determinants and focuses on the politics of resentment, voter volatility, overall disillusionment with the system and voter cynicism as a product of dissatisfaction with democratic politics. It focuses on the role of discontent with politics manifested in terms of cynicism and distrust. Emergence of demands that are no longer catered for by established parties, disillusionment with democracy, lack of confidence towards the political system (Ignazi 1992; Cutts et al. 2011) are associated with support for far right-wing parties. Betz (1993: 419) argues that far right-wing party success can be explained 'in part as a protest against the established political parties and their politics'. Vote for the far right is thus thought of as an act against the establishment. Voters express their dissatisfaction with democracy, their disapproval of mainstream parties and government policies.

As in the previous model, class, income and employment status are relevant predictors for far right-wing party support, but this is not related to objective measures. The model identifies as potential far right-wing voters those experiencing relative deprivation and the frustrations arising from this. These derive either from a comparison with one's own past or with social reference groups (Gurr 1970; Rydgren 2007). According to this model, class and partisan identities are no longer able to anchor voters onto mainstream parties, therefore enabling the far right to capitalise on protest politics by appealing to those who irrespective of social stratum see themselves as worse off. Another predictor relates to Eurosceptic attitudes. Far right-wing parties tend to adopt strong Eurosceptic positions, voicing concerns against European integration and EU policies (Vasilopoulou 2011). Voters who are disillusioned with

DOI: 10.1057/9781137535917.0007

the EU and its policies are more likely to opt for far right-wing parties. This theory expects protest to be directed against the freedom of labour and cultural mobility promoted by the EU, the resulting increase in immigration, multi-culturalism and competition for jobs with EU migrants (Halikiopoulou et al. 2012).[1]

Data and operationalisation

We employ data from the Hellenic Panel Component of the European Election Study 2014 (Andreadis et al. 2014). The European Election Study is an EU-wide post-election cross-sectional survey that monitors electoral participation and voting behaviour in European Parliament elections. The survey includes a number of questions that cover electoral behaviour, including specific questions on voting behaviour in the European Parliament elections, voting behaviour in the latest national elections, propensity to vote for specific parties; political attitudes, such as left-right orientation, attitudes on European integration, voters' subjective evaluations of party positions, satisfaction with democracy in the country and in the EU, government approval; and various socio-demographic characteristics including gender, income, occupation and education. The Greek component of the study was conducted as a web survey on a non-probability sample after the 2014 European Parliament elections. Post-stratification adjustments have been applied in order to reduce the bias of the estimates. The sample is representative in terms of gender, age, education, region and voting behaviour in the 2014 European Parliament elections (Andreadis 2014).

We test the two models outlined here, including (1) the socio-economic grievance model, which derives from the social cleavage approach, and (2) the political grievance model, which draws upon the partisan de-alignment approach. In order to test the socio-economic grievance model, we employ socio-economic variables including gender, age, levels of education, employment sector, employment status, place of residence and economic condition. *Gender* is a nominal variable with two categories; the remaining are nominal variables with multiple categories. We have constructed *age* as a categorical variable consisting of four age brackets: 18–25, 26–40, 41–64 and 65+. The age bracket 18–25 is the reference category. We expect the youngest and oldest categories

DOI: 10.1057/9781137535917.0007

of respondents to be the most likely to vote for the Golden Dawn. For *education*, we employ the categories included in the EES, which rely on the ISCED classifications. This measure provides information on respondents' higher level of education and consists of nine categories: (1) early childhood education; (2) primary; (3) lower secondary; (4) upper secondary; (5) post-secondary non-tertiary; (6) short cycle tertiary; (7) bachelor's or equivalent; (8) master's or equivalent; (9) doctoral or equivalent. We have recoded these into four categories: (1) low up to secondary (ISCED categories 1, 2, 3 and 4); (2) further/vocational (ISCED categories 5 and 6); (3) bachelor's or equivalent (ISCED category 7); and (4) master's and above (ISCED categories 8 and 9). Low up to secondary education serves as the reference category. We expect respondents that belong to the other categories to be less likely to opt for the Golden Dawn.

To capture where a person works, we use the variable *sector of main occupation*, which includes four categories: primary sector (agricultural, forestry, fisheries), secondary sector (industry: mining, construction, manufacturing), tertiary sector (transportation, communication, public utilities, services) and 'other', which encompasses occupations not captured by three other categories. We transformed the occupation variable into a set of dummies using secondary sector as a reference category. We expect people employed in the secondary sector category to be more likely to opt for the Golden Dawn. We also test whether *employment status* affects the likelihood to opt for the Golden Dawn. We include a variable that encompasses the following categories: (1) full-time; (2) part-time; (3) unemployed; (4) student; (5) retired; (6) housewife; (7) not in the labour force. Category 1 is our reference category. We expect that individuals who are employed part-time or are unemployed to be more likely to opt for the Golden Dawn compared to those who are in full-time employment. *Place of residence* has four categories, including rural area or village, small or middle-sized town, suburbs of large town or city and large town/city. We use the first category as reference and expect that probability to opt for the Golden Dawn increases in larger towns or cities. Economic condition is operationalised by *Income*. This is related to net household income and forms an objective evaluation of economic condition. It includes five categories: up to €10,000 per annum; €10,001–15,000 per annum; €15,001–25,000 per annum; €25,001–40,000 per annum; and over €40,000 per annum. Up to €10,000 is the first reference category.

DOI: 10.1057/9781137535917.0007

We expect people whose household income is lower than €10,000 to be more likely to opt for the Golden Dawn.

In order to test the explanatory value of the political grievance model, we employ variables that capture a number of attitudes. To capture *left-right* orientation, we use respondents' self-positioning on the left-right scale, 0 meaning 'left' and 10 meaning 'right'. Positions on *EU integration* are measured on a 0–10 scale, where 0 means that the unification of Europe has already gone too far and 10 means that European unification should be pushed further. The variable *dissatisfaction* captures whether an individual is satisfied with the way democracy works in Greece. This consists of two categories: satisfied and dissatisfied. We also include interaction terms between dissatisfaction with Greek democracy and position on the left-right dimension. Given that, in the crisis political environment, dissatisfied Greeks opted for left-wing parties as well, we argue that propensity to vote for the Golden Dawn with respect to dissatisfaction depends on an individual's position on the left-right dimension, with those dissatisfied Greeks on the right end of the spectrum more likely to opt for the Golden Dawn. The variable *government disapproval* consists of individuals' responses to the question 'Do you approve or disapprove of the government's record to date'. Since we are interested in those who are critical of the government's record, we have coded this into a dummy variable and predict Golden Dawn vote probability for those who disapprove. Here, we are also interested in respondents' subjective evaluation of changes in their own economic condition. To tap into this, we also use the variable *personal economic condition* compared to 12 months ago. Responses on this question were coded on a five-point Likert scale, such as 'much better', 'a little better', 'remained the same', 'a little worse', 'much worse'. Since we are mostly interested in the relationship between respondents' perception that their economic well-being has deteriorated and support for the Golden Dawn, we have recoded these into two categories: 'worse off', which includes 'a little worse' and 'much worse'; and 'not worse off' which includes 'much better', 'a little better' and 'remained the same'.

We have calculated two statistical models. The first tests the socio-economic grievance and the second the political grievance model. Our dependent variable is propensity to vote for the Golden Dawn based on responses to the question: 'We have a number of parties in Greece each of which would like to get your vote. How probable is it that you

DOI: 10.1057/9781137535917.0007

will ever vote for the popular association, Golden Dawn? Please express your views using a scale of 0 to 10, where 0 means "not at all likely" and 10 means "Very likely". You can use any number from 0 to 10'. We conceptualise our dependent variable as the probability of a given individual to opt for the Golden Dawn. We operationalise this as a proportion and have thus rescaled it to $0 < y < 1$. It is skewed towards smaller values (Obs = 1365; Mean = .0888722; Std. Dev. = .2467217). Given that our dependent variable of interest is continuous and restricted to the interval (0, 1), we estimate a beta regression model (Ferrari and Cribari-Neto 2004). The advantage of this model is also that it can accommodate lopsided distributions. This allows us to estimate the expected probability of a respondent to vote for the Golden Dawn conditional on a number of socio-demographic and attitudinal characteristics.

The Golden Dawn's prospective voter

Before proceeding to the findings we present an overview of the degree of overlap of voting propensities for the Golden Dawn and other Greek parties. We do this in order to gauge the ideological persuasions of prospective Golden Dawn voters by identifying what other parties they are likely to vote for. The voting propensity variable presupposes that citizens preselect a set of parties that they may opt for in the elections (Bochsler and Sciarini 2010). This represents their choice-set, which measures their expected utility from voting for each party on a scale from zero to ten. An analysis of the degree of overlap (see Appendix 1) shows that there is a statistically significant ordered relationship between propensity to vote for the Golden Dawn and propensity to vote for ANEL, Olive Tree and DIMAR. The association is negative for Olive Tree and DIMAR, meaning that those likely to vote for the Golden Dawn are highly unlikely to vote for these two parties; but positive for ANEL, entailing that those likely to vote for the Golden Dawn are also likely to vote for ANEL. The relationship is negative but not statistically significant with New Democracy, SYRIZA and KKE.

In terms of the actual analysis of voting propensity, we have tested both objective characteristics and subjective attitudes as possible predictors of Golden Dawn support. As far as socio-economic characteristics are concerned, the overall picture does not indicate clear patterns (see Table 3.1). Most socio-economic characteristics

DOI: 10.1057/9781137535917.0007

TABLE 3.1   *The impact of socio-economic characteristics on propensity to vote for the Golden Dawn*

	coeff.	s.e.
Female	−0.095	0.078
Age		
26–40	0.099	0.198
41–64	−0.07	0.202
65+	0.243	0.245
Education		
Further/vocational	−0.019	0.129
Bachelor or equivalent	−0.317***	0.109
Master and above	−0.363***	0.116
Sector of main occupation		
Primary	−0.441	0.276
Tertiary	−0.287**	0.136
Other	−0.270*	0.161
Employment status		
Part-time	−0.03	0.124
Unemployed	0.056	0.128
Student	−0.129	0.219
Retired	0.213	0.136
Housewife	0.504	0.366
Not in labour force	−0.017	0.178
Place of residence		
Small or middle-sized town	−0.043	0.172
Suburbs of large town or city	0.289	0.178
Large town/city	−0.029	0.159
Income		
€10,001–15,000	−0.089	0.125
€15,001–25,000	0.029	0.119
€25,001–40,000	−0.273**	0.131
Over €40,000	−0.199	0.167
Constant	−0.733**	0.314
Log likelihood	5131.915	
Wald chi^2	59.14	
Prob > chi^2	0.0001	
BIC	−10088.53	
N	1110	

Notes: * $p<.1$; ** $p<.05$; ***$p<.01$; Dependent variable: probability to vote for the Golden Dawn $0 < y < 1$.
Reference categories: Age: 18–25; Education: Low up to secondary;
Sector of main occupation: Secondary; Form of employment: Full-time;
Place of residence: Rural area or village; Income: Up to €10,000.

DOI: 10.1057/9781137535917.0007

do not appear to be associated with support for the Golden Dawn. In particular, gender, age, employment status and place of residence are not statistically significant. In other words, knowing whether an individual is female or male, young, middle-aged or old, employed part-time, full-time, is retired or is a student or a housewife or not in the labour force at all and whether an individual resides in a small, middle or large town or city is not helpful for understanding how likely they are to vote for the Golden Dawn. This is an interesting finding vis-à-vis literature on other far right-wing parties in Europe that finds that certain demographic characteristics, including gender and place of residence, are related to their support. For example, studies find that support for the BNP derives from older males residing in declining industrial towns (Ford and Goodwin 2010).

The findings are surprising, particularly in terms of gender, as most studies of the far right find that males are more likely supporters of far right-wing parties, especially when these parties are involved in violent activities. Givens (2004) finds that there is a gender gap in Austria and France but not in Denmark. This gap persists when controlling for other socio-economic and political variables. Mayer (1999) finds that women were less likely to opt for the Front National in the 1990s; although the gender gap seems to have narrowed in the first round of the 2012 French Presidential election (Mayer 2013). The findings on the Golden Dawn are consistent with literature that notes women's involvement in violent incidents (Psarras 2012: 420).

Regarding income, the findings are not consistent. The only income category that appears to make a difference compared to the baseline 'Up to €10,000' is '€25,001–40,000' indicating that those who fall within this category are least likely to vote for the Golden Dawn. The remaining income categories are not statistically significant, entailing that there is no clear correlation between income and support for the Golden Dawn. This finding is also interesting vis-à-vis the literature, as a number of studies tend to find that low income contributes to the explanation of far right-wing support. For example, Lubbers and Scheepers (2002) find that low income and deprivation are associated with support for the Front National. The association between low income and support for the Golden Dawn is more tenuous.

We find greater correlation with regard to occupation sector and levels of education. In particular, those who are employed in transportation, communication, public utilities and services (tertiary sector)

DOI: 10.1057/9781137535917.0007

are less likely to opt for the Golden Dawn compared to those mainly working class individuals who are employed in industry (secondary) sector. While these findings are consistent with the literature on occupation sector across Europe, it is important to note here the difference between Greece's type of economy and the secondary sector in the highly industrialised countries of Western Europe. Regarding levels of education, people with lowest education are more likely to vote for the Golden Dawn. Those with a bachelor's degree or equivalent and those with a master's degree or above are the least likely individuals to support the Golden Dawn (see Figure 3.1). These findings are consistent with other works that have examined propensity to vote for the far right (e.g., Swank and Betz 2002; Kitschelt 2007), for example, the Front National (Mayer 1999; Lubbers and Scheepers 2002) and UKIP (Ford and Goodwin 2014).

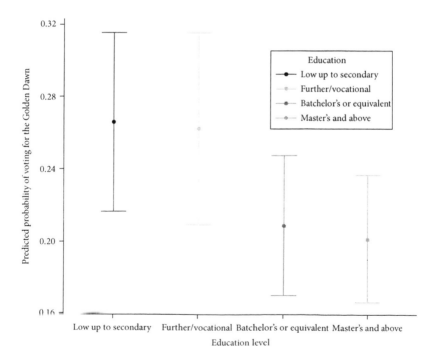

FIGURE 3.1   *Predicted probability of voting for the Golden Dawn at different levels of educational attainment*

Note: The bars represent 95% confidence intervals.

DOI: 10.1057/9781137535917.0007

The analysis of the impact of subjective attitudes on propensity to opt for the Golden Dawn indicates a clearer picture (Table 3.2). Attitudinal predictors associated with the political grievance model appear to have greater statistical significance. This indicates that factors such as disillusionment, dissatisfaction, EU position and relative deprivation, that is, the belief that one's condition is worse off compared to the past, are better predictors of Golden Dawn support.

Disapproval of the government's record is positively associated with support for the Golden Dawn. Dissatisfaction with the overall political system and the way democracy works in Greece is not statistically significant in itself, entailing that it is not a sufficient predictor for Golden Dawn support. When, however, this variable is interacted with an individual's position on the left-right dimension, it becomes statistically significant. In other words, those dissatisfied voters with a right-wing ideological persuasion are highly likely to vote for the Golden Dawn (Figure 3.2). Overall, the left-right dimension is important as the analysis indicates that the further right one's ideological belief is, the more likely they are to support the Golden Dawn. Finally, EU position is negatively related to Golden Dawn support. The more pro-EU a voter is, the less their propensity to opt for the Golden Dawn

TABLE 3.2   *The impact of attitudinal characteristics on propensity to vote for the Golden Dawn*

	coeff.	s.e.
Left-right self placement	0.128***	0.047
EU position	−0.058***	0.011
Dissatisfaction	−0.318	0.288
Dissatisfaction*Left-right self placement	0.085*	0.049
Government disapproval	0.483***	0.09
Personal economic condition: worse off	0.138*	0.075
Female	−0.081	0.07
Age	−0.003	0.003
Constant	4.646	5.22
Log likelihood	5633.6896	
Wald chi^2	179.13	
Prob > chi^2	0.000	
BIC	−11196.58	
N	1188	

Notes: * $p<.1$; ** $p<.05$; ***$p<.01$; Dependent variable: probability to vote for the Golden Dawn $0 < y < 1$. This model controls for age and gender.

DOI: 10.1057/9781137535917.0007

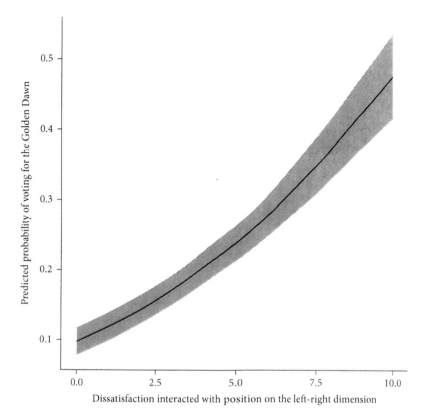

FIGURE 3.2 *Effect of dissatisfaction on the probability of voting for the Golden Dawn as position on the left-right dimension changes*

Note: The shaded areas represent 95% confidence intervals.

(Figure 3.3). These results are consistent with existing literature, which points to the relevance of attitudinal variables (e.g., Cutts et al. 2011; Van der Brug et al. 2013). Ford and Goodwin (2014) find that those most likely to vote for UKIP are those who, dissatisfied with mainstream parties, have been left behind and 'written out of the political debate'. These social groups had initially turned their backs to politics, but UKIP has changed this by offering them an outlet and a voice for their concerns.

Our findings show that Greek voters opted for the Golden Dawn because of and not despite its anti-systemic character, that is, the party's ability to claim issue ownership of anti-systemic politics framed within a

DOI: 10.1057/9781137535917.0007

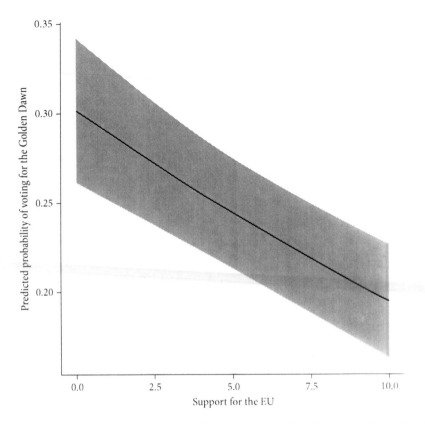

FIGURE 3.3   *Predicted probability of voting for the Golden Dawn at different levels of support for the EU*

Note: The shaded areas represent 95% confidence intervals.

nationalist populist rhetoric that targets mainstream parties and corruption. Protest is the prime cause for support for this party, cutting across objective socio-economic characteristics. Golden Dawn supporters appear to be disillusioned with mainstream political parties and seem to disregard the party's neo-Nazi, violent ideology. Indeed according to a supporter, 'The party has nothing to do with fascism now...it might have had originally but it has experienced a turnaround in the last years' (EU Observer 2014).

These findings are also confirmed when compared to actual vote criteria during the 2014 European Parliament elections (see Table 3.3). Dissatisfaction with the system is extremely high among Golden Dawn

DOI: 10.1057/9781137535917.0007

TABLE 3.3   *Main criteria for the selection of your vote choice in the recent elections (up to three answers)*

	GD supporters N=87	EES sample N=1042
The party that I feel closest to	33.9	55.5
The party with respected and experienced candidates	8.3	28
To overthrow the government and against the Memorandum	33.9	24.3
To support the government policies	0	10.3
With European criteria	1.3	25.8
In order to renew the political personnel of the country	33.6	34.2
To express my dissatisfaction with the entire political system	85	20.3

Source: Hellenic Panel Component of the European Election Study 2014 (Andreadis et al. 2014).

supporters at 85 per cent, which is significantly higher than the EES sample at 20.3 per cent. These data show that Golden Dawn supporters are protest voters who are expressing their disillusionment with the status quo. Golden Dawn supporters do not cast their vote in order to support government policies. Rather they have clear anti-systemic criteria when casting their vote. They wish to overthrow the government and are against the Memorandum of Understanding, which has set economic policy conditionality between Greece and its lenders.

Conclusion

Who is the prospective Golden Dawn voter? Part of the picture derived from the data is inconclusive, and we are unsure whether this voter is male or female, younger or older, employed, unemployed or a student and where this voter resides. We do know, however, that the Golden Dawn prospective voter is unlikely to have a university degree and is probably a school leaver or has graduated from a further education institution. Being employed in the secondary sector, this voter is likely to work in light or heavy industry. In the Greek context this means this voter could be a blue-collar worker involved in construction, operating machinery, industrial assembling and/or employed in shipyards. This

DOI: 10.1057/9781137535917.0007

voter is highly disaffected by the political system and has very little trust in the effectiveness of the government. Finally it is likely that this voter belongs to the right of the political spectrum and holds a very negative view of the EU.

How may we place this profile within the context of the Greek crisis and the sudden rise of the Golden Dawn? Drawing on literature on the impact of societal crises, we can argue that the crisis in Greece has created a cohort of 'losers' dissatisfied with the political system and democratic politics. Whether we see this in terms of socio-economic objective characteristics, such as the blue-collar workers of the secondary employment sector or the lowly educated who are more likely to be pushed out of better employment prospects given the scarcity of job opportunities; or subjective criteria such as comparing one's own situation to the past, these 'losers' are fundamentally disillusioned with the system. As per Lipset (1960), these may be the old middle classes who partly belong to the secondary employment sector such as self-employed craftsmen; or have a broader employment base but share a common belief that they can objectively still lose something (Minkenberg 2000). The key here is grievance, felt by those who are 'uprooted and threatened by social and economic change, whose position in society was being undermined, who had lost their traditional place, and were frightened of the future' (Carsten 1980: 232–233). What links these voters is their anxiousness, bewilderment, insecurity and resentfulness, which may prompt them to support a party that propagates a return to traditional values.

It would be limited to attribute this degree of disillusionment, insecurity and resentfulness to economic malaise alone. What differentiates the prospective Golden Dawn voter from the voters in other countries that have experienced economic malaise, such as Portugal, Ireland and Spain, who have mainly opted for punishing the incumbent, is the extent to which the crisis assumed a political and systemic character. Not only have Greek voters been disaffected by economic crisis, but most importantly the political and ideological crises that have accompanied it, culminating into a crisis of the nation-state, have exacerbated the extent to which these voters perceive themselves as the losers of a decadent failing system. Given the overall crisis of the Greek nation-state and its consequences on the foundations and legitimacy of the system itself, these voters are likely to opt for the Golden Dawn because of and not despite its anti-systemic character.

DOI: 10.1057/9781137535917.0007

The Golden Dawn's 'nationalist solution' is the party's response to political, social and economic misery. The return to a society of traditional values propagated by the Golden Dawn is presented as a solution to the problems of atomisation and isolation in crisis-ridden Greek society. Anti-systemic politics is presented as the solution to the problem of social decadence. Ultra-nationalism is presented as the basis on which to cleanse the internal and external elements that contribute to this social decadence. Finally, palingenensis is the presented as the ultimate solution: the rebirth of the nation out of the decadent state of the crisis, cleansed and transcendent of all social cleavages that contribute to social misery. The following chapters will provide an analysis of the Golden Dawn's nationalist solution by focusing on two interrelated myths in the party's discourse: social decadence and palingenensis.

Note

1　Another relevant attitudinal variable refers to anti-immigration attitudes. However, this is beyond the scope of this chapter, as the European Election Study 2014 does not include a relevant variable.

DOI: 10.1057/9781137535917.0007

4
The Myth of Social Decadence: The Golden Dawn's Populist Nation-Statism

Abstract: *This chapter focuses on the ways in which the Golden Dawn has shaped its own demand through its ideology, discourse and programmatic agenda. It examines the Golden Dawn's nationalist solution to the Greek crisis within the framework of fascist political myths and, more specifically, the myth of social decadence. The chapter first examines fascism and the myth of social decadence from a theoretical perspective. It proceeds by contextualising the ideological components of this myth in the discourse and the programmatic agenda of the Golden Dawn by breaking down its populist nation-statism—as the key answer to the social decadence problem—into the following fascist principles: popular supremacy, paramilitarism/violence, transcendence and cleansing.*

Keywords: discourse; fascist myths; ideology; programmatic agenda; social decadence

Vasilopoulou, Sofia and Daphne Halikiopoulou. *The Golden Dawn's 'Nationalist Solution': Explaining the Rise of the Far Right in Greece.* New York: Palgrave Macmillan, 2015. DOI: 10.1057/9781137535917.0008.

DOI: 10.1057/9781137535917.0008

Introduction

This chapter focuses on supply and, more specifically, on the ways in which the Golden Dawn has capitalised on favourable demand-side conditions and shaped its own demand through its ideology, discourse and programmatic agenda. We understand the success of the Golden Dawn as dependent on the extent to which it was able to propound plausible solutions to the three sets of crises—economic, political and ideological—that befell Greece and culminated in an overall crisis of the nation-state. To this the Golden Dawn offered a nationalist solution, striving to 'forge social rebirth based on a holistic-national radical third way' (Mann 2004: 11). We define the Golden Dawn as a fascist, and more specifically neo-Nazi, group characterised by the principles of nationalism, statism, paramilitarism, transcendence and cleansing (Mann 2004). Nationalism is at the core of the party's ideology. The Greek nation is an organic entity defined by ascriptive criteria, such as bloodline, language, religion and community of birth. Greek status cannot be acquired; it is something one is born into. Nationalism overrides all other political allegiances, including left and right. The Golden Dawn emphasises resistance against pluralism and democratic rule, as these are seen as a threat to national sovereignty, unity and authentic popular supremacy. The party's proposed populist nation-statism is seen as the only type of authentic democratic rule that could protect the sovereignty of the Greek nation and embody the collective will of the people. Violence through paramilitary means is justified so long as it protects this regime. In this way the Golden Dawn seeks to transcend social cleavages, which are seen as artificial divisions created by liberal democracy and bringing about social decay. It is essential to cleanse the nation from all elements that bring about this social degeneration. The party emphasises the divine duty to physically eliminate enemies and on the necessity of sacrifice for this ultimate goal. Purging is directed to those outsiders and insiders that seek to undermine the purity of the Greek nation, engendering its decline.

This book places the Golden Dawn's nationalist solution within the framework of fascist political myths (Griffin 1991) and, more specifically, the twin myths of social decadence and palingenesis. This chapter focuses on the former and examines the party's ideological premise that the current system has degenerated into a system of social decay. The Golden Dawn's emphasis on the social decadence myth is a characteristic the

DOI: 10.1057/9781137535917.0008

party shares with fascist movements and forms the starting point—and legitimation—of the party's nation-statism, paramilitarism, transcendence and cleansing. The party lauds ' "resistance", "will", "movement", "collective action", "the masses", and the dialectic of "progress" through "struggle", "force", and "violence" ' (Mann 2004: 6). This dialectic is characterised by progress instigated by the Golden Dawn, not in elitist terms, but rather as the embodiment of the popular will of the people to end the current rotten system and substitute it with the authentic rule of the people through a nationalist movement from below.

In this chapter we first examine fascism and the myth of social decadence from a theoretical perspective. We proceed by contextualising the ideological components of this myth in the discourse and the programmatic agenda of the Golden Dawn. We do this by breaking down the Golden Dawn's populist nation-statism—as the key answer to the social decadence problem—into the following fascist principles: popular supremacy, paramilitarism/violence, transcendence and cleansing. We carry out our analysis through a qualitative examination of Golden Dawn's online materials; more specifically in this chapter we have examined the sections on 'ideology, identity and political positions', as well as over 1,000 texts in the 'news' section of the party's website.

Fascism and the myth of social decadence

Fascism, it is often argued, has neither systematic theory nor a distinctive social base. In their definition of fascism, scholars often include what such movements tend to negate. For example, Juan Linz (1976: 12) has described fascism as 'anti-parliamentary, anti-liberal, anti-communist, populist and therefore anti-proletarian, partly anti-capitalist and anti-bourgeois, anti-clerical or at least, non-clerical'. Breuilly (1993: 290) defines fascism as a 'radical, anti-bourgeois, anti-liberal, anti-marxist' movement. Beyond its negations, scholars have identified key ideological features of fascist movements including 'nationalism, authoritarian statism, corporatism and syndicalism, imperialism, idealism, voluntarism, romanticism, mysticism, militarism, and violence' (Payne 1980). Mann (2004) adds transcendence and cleansing, while Breuilly (1993: 290) terms it a 'movement of nationalist-imperialist integration'. Eatwell (2001) has identified four key characteristics of fascism including

DOI: 10.1057/9781137535917.0008

nationalism, holism, radicalism, and the third way. Scholars have also defined fascism in terms of its minimum, usually encompassing certain ideological features (Griffin 1991; Rydgren 2007). Nolte (1965) identified this minimum as combining anti-Marxism, anti-liberalism and anti-conservatism. Griffin (1991) identifies this ideological minimum in terms of three mythic components aimed at generating internal cohesion: 'populist ultra-nationalism, the myth of decadence, and the rebirth myth'.

While definitions of fascist movements vary, we may identify two overall themes that are recurrent: the first is the theme of societal degeneration and decay; and the second is the proposed fascist solution which encompasses the necessity for national rebirth through a collective movement from below, usually embodied by a fascist party. We adopt Griffin's (1991) decadence myth as a theoretical framework for explaining the starting point of fascism's nationalist solution. We trace the dialectical process from degenerate social condition to the purging of impure elements in order to arrive to the ultimate goal of national purification and rebirth, through Mann's (2004) analysis which focuses on nationalism, paramilitarism, statism, transcendence, and cleansing as the key features of fascism.

Fascism is often described as the product of a crisis of modernity. In other words, as a movement triggered by crisis conditions, for example, the Great War or the Great Depression or the rapid transition to democratisation. According to Mann (2004), inter-war fascism was the response to four sets of crises—political, ideological, economic and military—and an attempt to seize these four sources of social power. The concept of decadence is linked to the concept of societal crisis and to the idea that fascism is an alternative modernity (Eatwell 2001). We may deduce that it applies to an overall worldview—that is, the decay that encompasses all forms of social life including moral, cultural, political, as well as a decline of power. This decay is caused, partially, by bourgeois democracy and the increasing atomisation of society and materialism that accompany it, while its communist and socialist alternatives are equally decadent. Only fascism 'could "transcend" the moral decay and class conflict of bourgeois society with a "total plan" offering a statist "third way" between capitalism and socialism' (Mann 2004: 7).

What is this third way? Fascist movements adopt a number of mechanisms for social purification. We examine these in terms of the

DOI: 10.1057/9781137535917.0008

aforementioned themes in Mann's (2004) analysis, including national-ism, statism, transcendence, cleansing, and paramilitarism. A detailed account of nationalism and the ultimate goal of national rebirth (the palingenetic myth) is provided in the next chapter. Here we focus on the remaining four features, which relate to the myth of social decadence. Fascists seek social purification through a populist nation-statism, or in other words a statism justified as a popular movement from below. Support for an authoritarian type of democracy is legitimated by virtue of the nationalist leader being the mirror of the nation and its people. The fascist party, and in more accurate terms the leader of the fascist party, is not above or next to the people, nor the representative of the people, but rather the embodiment of the people and their collective will. Fascism therefore relies on popular supremacy and the single will of the collec-tive, which constitutes the authentic rule of the people. Inherent to this is the transcendence of social cleavages: the single will of the collective may only be achieved through transcendence, and in turn this requires the elimination of all political divisions. As mentioned earlier, the targets include liberal democracy and hence bourgeois elements, as well as communism, socialism, and proletarian elements. This alludes to the concept of cleansing the nation defined as a struggle against all regimes, movements, social groups or individuals described as the enemies of the nation. These may be understood as the internal enemies, that is, the political elites mentioned earlier; or external enemies, that is, the foreign elements contributing to moral and cultural decay, for example, people of Jewish origin during inter-war Europe. Violence is the key for achieving cleansing; and, hence, the adoption of paramilitarism as both an ideal and a form of party organisation and activism. Military power and, by extension, the army are portrayed by fascist movements as the ultimate forces for the preservation of the nation and the achievement of social purity. Fascism is characterised by the '"bottom-up" and violent quality of its paramilitarism' (Mann 2004: 16) and 'entwined with the other two main fascist power resources: in electoral struggle and in the undermining of elites' (Mann 2004: 17).

The Golden Dawn's populist nation-statism

Among current far right-wing parties in Western Europe, the Golden Dawn is the one that most resembles fascism, and in particular

DOI: 10.1057/9781137535917.0008

traditional Nazism, in its outright espousal of National Socialism. Its symbol is the Meander which, despite its striking resemblance to the swastika, the Golden Dawn claims is an ancient Greek symbol (Golden Dawn 2012d). The party rejects liberalism and socialism and endorses what it terms the 'third biggest ideology in history', that is, nationalism, combined with support for an all-powerful state premised on 'popular sovereignty' (Golden Dawn 2012b). In its manifesto the party states that being a member of the Golden Dawn entails the acceptance of the following principles: the establishment of the state in accordance with nationalism; the moral obligations that derive from this ideology, including the rejection of any authority that perpetuates societal decline; the acceptance of nationalism as the only authentic revolution; the establishment of the popular state in which there are no inequalities on the basis of wealth (Golden Dawn 2012c); racial supremacy and more specifically the belief in the continuation of the 'Greek race' from antiquity to the modern day; the idea that the state must correspond and be subservient to the nation/race; and the nationalisation of all institutions (Golden Dawn 2012d). The party defines itself as an ideological movement guided by the principle of popular nationalism (Golden Dawn 2012a). Ideology for the Golden Dawn is more than a system of beliefs. It is a way of life and a worldview understood as an inevitable and conscious struggle for the party's beliefs. The party identifies its members as 'conscious political soldiers' who are obligated to fight for its ideals (Golden Dawn 2012d: 11).

We place the Golden Dawn within the fascist theoretical framework and analyse its main ideological tenets in terms of the social decadence myth. The ideological principles outlined in the Golden Dawn's manifesto link the party to traditional fascist—and more specifically Nazi—principles. Nationalism—defined by the Golden Dawn as the supremacy of the 'ethnos-race'; statism—the establishment of the state in accordance to nationalism (which is supreme); paramilitarism—the support for struggle and violence in order to achieve Golden Dawn ideals and the definition of its members as soldiers; transcendence—the establishment of the popular state in which there are no inequalities; and cleansing—the moral obligation to eliminate any authority that perpetuates social decline. There is a distinction here between cleansing from within, referring to the internal enemies of the nation, including people of all different ideologies, and cleansing from external enemies, referring to immigrants or those of non-Greek origin.

DOI: 10.1057/9781137535917.0008

A movement from 'below'

The starting point for the Golden Dawn (2012d: 2) is social decay.

> Hellenism is on a downward slope [...] the economic crisis is the tip of the iceberg. Behind it lies a decline of Values, an unprecedented political decline, a political bankruptcy, the decline of a whole nation, the Great Nation of the Greeks. Many worked towards this decline for decades. These are not only foreigners, but also some Greek speakers. That is, only Greek speakers, but not Greeks, because a Greek is only the one that has Greek consciousness.

The party sees itself at the helm of a movement whose vocation is to purify the Greek nation from social decadence associated with corruption, deception, partisan interests and cleptocracy (Golden Dawn 30/05/2014). The Golden Dawn criticises the current (and past) Greek government(s) for contributing to social, moral and cultural decay. The country is in 'ruins' because of the incompetence of Greek politicians who 'destroyed the nation' (Golden Dawn 3/01/2014). We are living in a 'dark, miserable and degenerate era dominated by loansharks and their slaves' (Golden Dawn 12/08/2013). The constitution and the MPs are a 'disease' (Golden Dawn 31/07/2013), while society is governed by the 'political hubris of the puppets of the regime' (Golden Dawn 20/11/2013a) whose 'cheap interests have destroyed the national economy and ruined the education system, the health system, and Greek civilization' (Golden Dawn 2012d: 4) and 'threaten the survival of our nation' (6).

According to the Golden Dawn, authentic democracy in Greece is 'self-destructing' (Golden Dawn 15/07/2013) because it has 'abused the right to freedom and equality by teaching Greek citizens to interpret audacity as a right, unlawfulness as a freedom, impudence as an equality and anarchy as a joy [...] it is distorted and eroded, having become identified with greed, disobedience and the erosion of all Principles and Values' (Golden Dawn 15/07/2013). This societal malaise is resulting in the atomisation of Greek society and in the 'slavery and degeneration of its people and its civilization' (Golden Dawn 15/07/2013).

Therefore, the decadence of Greek society is all encompassing: it is political, cultural, moral and a decline of power, that is, Greece's underdog status compared to its Golden Past. It is the party's calling to lead the Greek people in a difficult struggle towards 'Virtue and self-improvement' (Golden Dawn 30/05/2014). This can only be materialised through a 'National government with a coherent plan and socio-political vision aligned with the principles of Nationalism and popular socialism'

DOI: 10.1057/9781137535917.0008

(Golden Dawn 06/03/2013). Only the type of state that adheres to these principles 'and which serves these eternal revolutionary principles of the Nationalist Worldview will result to the final goal of the formation of a new society and a new type of man' (Golden Dawn 2012b).

The party envisages itself as the embodiment of the collective will of the Greek people and seeks ultimate state power, which it understands as the epitome of the nation and its will. The Golden Dawn sees itself not in elitist terms, but rather as a movement from below. 'The Nationalist Socialist leader does not stand above or beside the people, he is not part of the people, he is the People' (*Efimerida ton Sydakton* 2013). He incarnates the secret 'calling of the blood', and his ultimate goal is full control of state power in the name of the nation. The party's organisational structures reflect this. Within the organisation of the Golden Dawn the leader is supreme. The party understands the 'bourgeois' concept of majority rule as hypocritical and also rejects the 'Bolshevik principle of the proletarian masses'. As supporters of 'the third biggest ideology in history', Golden Dawn members take upon them the responsibility and duty to remain loyal to the supreme 'principle of the leader' (*Efimerida ton Sydakton* 2013). The leader of the party aspires to be the leader of the nation, embodying the singular will of the masses.

For the Golden Dawn, representative democracy is not the 'true democracy' of the people (Golden Dawn 12/06/2014). Representative democracy is 'the child of capitalism', an instrument through which capitalism dominates the popular masses. It is the tool through which capitalism portrays its will as the popular will (Golden Dawn 04/08/2012). For this reason the party condemns liberal democracy and its institutions and in turn admires fascist and totalitarian regimes. Its members glorify fascist personalities, portraying them as heroes for purifying their nations and for epitomising the will of people in a truly democratic system. Party materials make ample references to fascists such as Greece's Ioannis Metaxas and Spain's Jose Antonio Primo de Rivera and Francisco Franco (Golden Dawn 20/11/2013b).

The ideal regime for Greece, according to the Golden Dawn, is the August 4th Regime, led by Ioannis Metaxas between 1936 and 1941. During the August 4th Regime, 'Greece became an anti-communist, anti-parliamentarian and totalitarian state with an agricultural and working class base, and hence an anti-plutocratic state. The country was not ruled by one party; the party was embodied by the whole people, except the unrepentant communists and the reactionary elements of

DOI: 10.1057/9781137535917.0008

the old regime' (Golden Dawn 01/05/2013). Metaxas's contribution to the welfare state is emphasised with frequent descriptions of a number of popular economic policies the dictator introduced, including the establishment of the welfare state and the introduction of national insurance; a six day working week; and the minimum wage. Metaxas also established collective Labour agreements 'helping to eradicate unemployment' (e.g., Golden Dawn 04/08/2012, 28/10/2012, 01/05/2013, 06/08/2013, 06/04/2014). It is a duty of the Golden Dawn to 'strive for the attribution of historical justice for Metaxas, whose historical contribution to Greece has often been distorted by plutocrats' (Golden Dawn 06/08/2013).

The Golden Dawn's relationship with the Greek 1967–1974 junta regime is complex. Besides some ideological differences, and despite some well-known links between the Golden Dawn and the members of the Colonels' regime, the party selectively mentions the junta in its materials. The Golden Dawn is also careful not to glorify Hitler and Nazism, as part of the party's strategy to disassociate itself from German Nazism. The latter is vilified in Greece for the obvious reasons of invasion and subsequent occupation during the 1940s. Metaxas on the other hand, is associated in popular imagery with the legendary 'No' of 28 October 1940, that is, Greece's refusal to co-operate with Nazi Germany and its subsequent invasion. Metaxas therefore is a contradictory figure in Greek history, already institutionalised as a hero for his historic defiance of German aggression, while 28 October is celebrated and commemorated annually as a national holiday. The Golden Dawn puts forward a discourse that glorifies a Greek politician who, on the one hand, is a fascist, but, on the other, is publicly recognised as an important personality of 20th-century Greek history, both for some of his labour policies but most importantly for his 'heroic defiance' of the Nazis. 'Metaxas placed national independence, as well the Dignity and Interest of the Greek people above foreign interests, regardless of the power with which they tried to impose their domination' (Golden Dawn 29/01/2014).

This rampant nation-statism and emphasis on welfare is also evident in the party's activities. Accompanying its criticism of Greek democracy, the Golden Dawn is actively attempting to offer an alternative service of state and welfare provisions in line with its ideal to encompass all aspects of social life. The party organised numerous welfare provision activities, including the organisation of job centres (Golden Dawn 28/09/2012), blood donations and 'soup kitchens' intended only for Greeks, a status

DOI: 10.1057/9781137535917.0008

to be confirmed by the presentation of a Greek identity card to one of the Golden Dawn members on site. The party has also set up a health provision service in order to support Greek people 'at a time when the national health care system is in decay and medical care is shrinking' (Golden Dawn 05/12/2012). The party's social solidarity programme is directed especially towards vulnerable social groups, who are not protected by the state. Funding for these activities is claimed to derive from the Golden Dawn MPs' salaries, thus alluding to the ultimate ideals of sacrifice, selflessness, and popular supremacy that define the party's fascist ideology.

Internal and external enemies: transcendence and cleansing

The party's key goal is to transcend social cleavages internally and cleanse the nation ethnically. It identifies middle-class complacency, liberal democracy, and communism (Breuilly 1993) as the 'enemies from within'. Those that do not share the biological features of the Greeks are the external enemies. The Golden Dawn's rejection of both liberal democracy and communism is in line with the fascist ideological principles of transcendence and cleansing. True democracy, and by extension a system which embodies the collective will of the people, require the elimination of all political divisions. This is consistent with the Golden Dawn's declaration that it is the proponent of the third biggest ideology in history, that is, nationalism. The Golden Dawn seeks 'catharsis' and is perpetually engaged 'in a Manichaean demonization of its enemies' (Eatwell 1996: 313). The party rejects all authority 'whether stemming from a dictatorship of military-economic interests, or a dictatorship of parliamentarism. These are the two sides of the same coin' (Golden Dawn 2012b). The primary Golden Dawn policy aim is 'national independence', or 'to free the country from the agents of foreign interests that have governed Greece during the *metapolitefsi* era' (Golden Dawn 2012c). This is how the party justifies its anti-communist and anti-liberal democratic stance: these cleavages are artificial, and they serve foreign interests and bring about social decay. The Golden Dawn pledges to 'destroy' the old 'rotten system', which it associates with stagnation and corruption. Its cause is a struggle between the 'pure' Greek nationalists versus the 'evil' others and their internal collaborators, that is, those Greek politicians who have, and continue to, support it in order to profit financially. Social degeneration is as much the doing of internal as it

DOI: 10.1057/9781137535917.0008

is of external elites—and their 'anti-Hellenic' policies—including the European Union, Germany, the United States and international Zionism. Modern Greece is always presented as an underdog in contrast to its former imperial glory, which must be restored. It is essential to cleanse the nation from all internal and external elements that contribute to social degeneration. Either external or internal, these enemies are forces that seek the eradication of the Greek nation. Golden Dawn materials are replete with such references.

Communists are identified as those internationalists that seek the annihilation of the Greek nation. Communism is despised for its internationalism and inherent opposition to the concept of the nation-state. Communists are portrayed as traitors of the nation (Golden Dawn 15/09/2013) who represent a risk to 'the ethnic and racial homogeneity of the Greek nation' (Golden Dawn 29/08/2013). They are historically responsible for terrorism (Golden Dawn 4/12/2013), assassinations (Golden Dawn 2/08/2013), and treason (Golden Dawn 01/08/2013). Liberal democracy is a despised 'child of capitalism' and a tool for exploitation. In fact, the Golden Dawn describes Greece's democratic regime as a 'junta' that rules without true legitimacy but rather through imposition by 'corrupt' and 'incompetent puppets', who serve their self-interest. It is these politicians that led Greece to 'ethnocide', by accepting the terms and conditions of the Memorandum of Understanding and locking Greece into a contract of unpopular austerity measures. Greece's democratic regime is described as a 'sinful status quo'. In fact, all the events that are unfolding in Greece 'constitute the natural development of a series of foolish and treacherous policies! (The policies) of an oligarchy that literally gambled our country in the name of cheap partisan interests' (Golden Dawn 2012d: 3).

Contributing to this ethnocide are also Greece's external enemies, 'the foreign loan sharks, contractors, pimps, media owners and illegal immigrants' (Golden Dawn 07/01/2014) to whom the internal collaborators have sold the country out. International Zionism, the United States and the Troika (the IMF and European elites) are all also part of an international conspiracy against the Greeks: 'the Greek people and a movement, the Golden Dawn, are standing before the monster which seeks to devour motherland and the people' (Golden Dawn 27/12/2013). The bailout and subsequent austerity measures are not nothing but 'an experiment to impose the IMF's ethnocidal measures in a nominal democracy' (Golden Dawn 27/12/2013).

DOI: 10.1057/9781137535917.0008

Propaganda and violence

The Golden Dawn seeks to legitimise cleansing of its internal and external enemies through its propaganda. The party attempts to 'create a new political culture' (Eatwell 1996: 312) by spreading its message as widely as possible. It was revealed in 2014 that the hierarchy of the organisation publishes internal documents containing the 'propagandist line of the party', which all members must adhere to (*To Vima* 2014). The Golden Dawn's propagandist machinery is elaborate containing various techniques. The dissemination of their information is highly organised and includes printed and online media. Their printed materials include their newspapers 'Golden Dawn', 'Forward' (*Εμπρός*) and 'Target' (*Στόχος*). They are also available on the party's website. The latter also includes televised broadcasts by Golden Dawn members, as well as a number of sub-links detailing the party's 'ideology, identity and political stance'; the contact details of various Golden Dawn-related local organisations; information on the party's youth branch; speeches, interviews, and biographical notes on the leader; speeches and questions to the Greek Parliament; and information on Golden Dawn's MEPs, as well as local councillors. The Golden Dawn's website contains a very elaborate 'news' section, which includes ideological texts on history and civilisation, and a link to the party's multi-media section, which includes broadcasts and various interviews.

All these materials emphasise Greece's social decay and the need for cleansing by targeting those internal and external elites who are responsible for the country's social, moral, economic and political degeneration. The Golden Dawn seeks to achieve cleansing through violence. Militarism hence is the key to both the Golden Dawn's ideology and organisational structures and is ingrained in politics. 'The army is the ultimate value. A value that encloses within it blood, struggle and sacrifice. It is the Honour of the Uniform. The great leaders in history never removed their army uniform in order to wear politician's outfit' (Golden Dawn 09/10/2014). The Golden Dawn admires the army, not only because of its institutional significance as protector of national security, but also symbolically as the embodiment of the ultimate value of collective sacrifice for the nation. 'The army, for us all, was, is and will be something supreme and something special […] it is a worldview' (Golden Dawn 09/10/2014). In its justification for the supremacy of the army, the party offers an overview of the role of the Greek army from

DOI: 10.1057/9781137535917.0008

antiquity until the present day in what it perceives to be a perennial Greek nation. The army 'summarises all armed combats from antiquity until today' including 'the battle of Marathon, the battle of Salamina, Leonidas' 300, Constantine of Byzantium, the 1821 Greek war of independence, the fight for Macedonia, the Balkan wars, the epic of 1940 and the struggle for Cyprus' (Golden Dawn 09/10/2014).

The party's members see themselves as 'street soldiers' fighting for the nationalist cause. The act automatically implies 'valour', 'bravery', 'honour', 'self-sacrifice', a 'superhuman strength and dignity', all inherent traits of the Greeks (e.g., Golden Dawn 14/07/2013, 19/08/2013, 04/09/2013). Admiring the army as the 'natural aristocracy of the people' (Golden Dawn 08/11/2014) requires army-like demeanour: discipline, ultimate respect for the leader, uniformed marching and saluting. This places violence at the heart of Golden Dawn's activities and illustrates their distinctive view of democracy as a bourgeois construct only to be used as a means for achieving their ultimate goal: its abolition (Michaloliakos 2013). It also explains the link between Golden Dawn members and army officials, as well as the organisation of 'paramilitary orders' or 'battalions' (τάγματα εφόδου).

The term 'paramilitary orders' or 'battalions' alludes to the paramilitary wing of the Nazi party. As far as the Golden Dawn is concerned, this term is used to describe the party's regional and/or local paramilitary groupings that have been termed responsible for the Golden Dawn's violent acts in the past 20 years. Also known as 'Phalanx', 'Golden Eagles' or 'Protesilaus', these paramilitary groupings have a hierarchical structure, receive army-like training and are in possession of various weapons and plan organised attacks against political (e.g., left-wing) targets, as well as immigrants irrespective of origin (*Kathimerini* 2014). They also offer protection. The party's paramilitary activity came under investigation after the murder of Pavlos Fyssas and the subsequent imprisonment of Golden Dawn members in late 2013. As of the time of writing, various case files released between late 2013 and late 2014 revealed a heightened paramilitary activity including 'army camps', training and possession of illegal weapons.

Conclusion

In this chapter, we have examined the Golden Dawn's ideology, organisation and programmatic agenda through the lens of the fascist

DOI: 10.1057/9781137535917.0008

social decadence myth. We have shown that the party may be placed within the fascist and more specifically within the neo-Nazi theoretical framework, by focusing on its core ideological tenets including statism, paramilitarism, transcendence, and cleansing. The key justification is the myth of social decadence, or in other words the fascist premise, that that society is in decline and may only be reborn through a statist movement from below, which will transcend social cleavages and cleanse the nation internally and externally. The Golden Dawn centres its rhetoric against the old 'rotten system', which is upheld by politicians associated with stagnation, corruption and collaboration with exploitative foreign powers. These politicians, whether communists or proponents of the centre right or the centre left, constitute the party's internal enemies. In addition, foreign powers, including the United States, Germany, the IMF, the European Union and 'international Zionism', as well as immigrants of all origins are also responsible for the social, economic, political and moral degeneration of Greece. It is through this cleansing that the nation will arise from its ashes, reborn and purged of all impure elements.

Ultra-nationalism is one of the key ideological components of the Golden Dawn. The Golden Dawn emphasises the superiority of Greek Orthodox descent, Greece's unique language and ancient heritage and the glorification of struggle against the other, which is portrayed as aggressive and expansionist but culturally inferior. Greek identity is contrasted against the Ottomans (or any non-Western region) on the basis of Christianity versus Islam; and the Greek language as an ancient language of a high civilisation versus the 'dark years' and backwardness of Ottoman imperial rule. The Greek nation is portrayed as under threat and constantly undergoing an ideological battle to be salvaged from destruction. The concept of threat is fundamental to this dichotomy. However, what makes the Golden Dawn a fascist formation is not simply its ultra-nationalism, which is a characteristic of all far right-wing parties in general, but more specifically the theme of palingenesis. It is this myth of national rebirth or Phoenix-like resurrection of the nation that is the key theme of the next chapter. In summary, we focus on the Golden Dawn's 'nationalist solution' to social decadence through an analysis of the myth of palingenesis and calls for ethnic election.

DOI: 10.1057/9781137535917.0008

5
The Myth of National Rebirth: The Golden Dawn's Populist Ultra-nationalism

Abstract: *This chapter focuses on the second component of the Golden Dawn's nationalist solution, namely, the fascist myth of national rebirth. The chapter places the Golden Dawn's palingenetic vision within the framework of ethnic election and examines the ways in which the party draws upon available cultural reservoirs. Its main proposition is that the Greek crisis offered fertile ground for the Golden Dawn to present itself as the saviour of the nation and defender of the national mission. We show that this type of nationalism forms the Golden Dawn's master narrative and argue that the party's success is partly related to its ability to claim ownership of nationalist issues through employing a narrative of chosenness and ethnic election.*

Keywords: chosenness; ethnic election; fascist myths; national rebirth

Vasilopoulou, Sofia and Daphne Halikiopoulou. *The Golden Dawn's 'Nationalist Solution': Explaining the Rise of the Far Right in Greece.* New York: Palgrave Macmillan, 2015. DOI: 10.1057/9781137535917.0009.

DOI: 10.1057/9781137535917.0009

Introduction

This chapter focuses on the second component of the Golden Dawn's nationalist solution, namely, the myth of palingenesis (Griffin 1991) and the party's emphasis on national rebirth as the solution to Greece's moral, cultural, economic, political and social decay. The fascist myth of palingenetic ultra-nationalism constitutes a key ideological premise underpinning the party's rhetoric and programmatic agenda. The solution to social decadence is a 'phoenix-like' national rebirth from the ashes of the old degenerate order. We understand the Golden Dawn's palingenetic vision through the framework of chosenness and ethnic election (Smith 1999) and examine the ways in which the party draws upon available cultural reservoirs in its emphasis on national rebirth. In particular, we focus on four aspects of ethnic election: a constant reinforcement of a strict boundary between the ethnic community and the other; a sense of moral superiority over outsiders; a doctrine of spiritual liberation that emphasises the community's special destiny and tends to include a radical reversal from its current underdog status; and the necessity of an elite-driven mobilisation (Smith 1999). Our main proposition is that the Greek crisis has offered fertile ground for the Golden Dawn to present itself as the saviour of the nation and defender of the national mission. We show that this type of nationalism forms the Golden Dawn's master narrative and argue that the party's success is partly related to its ability to claim ownership of nationalist issues through employing a narrative of palingenesis, chosenness and ethnic election. The party's ability to legitimate its statism, cleansing and support for violence through nationalism is at the heart of its appeal, partly explaining why it has been capable of attracting a broad electoral base.

In this chapter we first examine the role nationalism plays in far right-wing party discourse and ideology. On the one hand, the aim is to place the far right within the theoretical ethnic-civic framework in the study of nationalism often used to explain the nativistic framework of far right-wing parties (Mudde 2007; Hainsworth 2008; Halikiopoulou et al. 2013). On the other hand, we aim to show that the ideology and discourse of the Golden Dawn goes beyond the framework of ethnic nationalism to include a focus on the myth of palingenesis which we examine through the prism of chosenness and ethnic election. We proceed to analyse the role of the nation within Golden Dawn's ideology and then place the party's mobilisation appeals within the national awakening framework.

DOI: 10.1057/9781137535917.0009

We do so through a qualitative analysis of Golden Dawn's online materials; more specifically in this chapter we have examined 504 Golden Dawn online materials that refer to Greek history, uploaded on the Golden Dawn website under the section 'History-Civilization' during the period 29 April 2012–15 July 2014.

Nationalism and far right-wing parties

Nationalist doctrine provides the basis for the legitimacy of the modern nation-state. The key is the congruence between state and nation: nationalism is a type of social contract guarded by the state and binding those who belong to the same nation in a solidarity pact (Wimmer 1997). The core doctrine of nationalism emphasises the ultimate values of freedom and national self-determination. It assumes that the world consists of sovereign, individual and distinct nations with their own history and culture. Because the nation is the ultimate source of sovereignty, loyalty to it must override all other loyalties. Given that self-determination is the ultimate goal, peace may only be achieved if every nation is free and secure. The obvious controversy implied in this premise is what constitutes a nation and why some nations and nationalisms are defined by different criteria to others. Hence the premise of the 'nationalist Janus' (Kohn 1946; Nairn 1975; Smith 1991; Hechter 2000), the thesis that nationalism is a double-faceted ideology. It may sometimes appear 'as an absolutist creed which generates intolerance and violence, while other times it takes a liberal form, offering individual liberation within a community of citizens' (Brown 1999: 281).

The double-faceted character of nationalism has been theorised in the field in terms of the 'ethnic-civic' distinction, that is, the broad characterisation of nations and nationalisms as either exclusive, organic and defined by ascriptive criteria or as inclusive, voluntaristic and defined by institutional criteria. Meinecke's classic dichotomy between *culturnation* and *staatsnation* has been formulated into the ethnic and civic distinction between those nations and nationalisms that are genealogical, based on blood, creed and common ancestry and often being described as irrational and radical; and those that are liberal and voluntarist, based on territory, the law, the economy, citizenship and a common political idea (Kohn 1946; Smith 1991; Brown 1999). This broad theoretical perspective has been used to explain the different manifestations of

DOI: 10.1057/9781137535917.0009

nationalism worldwide, for example, why nationalism became associated with fascism in Germany and liberalism in the West. Kohn (1946) stressed the close relationship between nationalism, the Enlightenment and liberalism, that is, the civic Western variant, which ought not to be equated with the ethnic nationalism of the East, manifested in its worst form in German Nazism (Calhoun 2007: 118).

While this distinction refers to ideal types and has been criticised on a number of grounds (Smith 1991; Brown 1999; Zimmer 2003; Kaufmann 2002, Brubaker 2003), it may however be useful analytically in order to deconstruct elements of the ideology of far right-wing parties. Scholars identify a close relationship between ethnic nationalism and the far right because of its emphasis on the supremacy of the homogeneous nation (Hainsworth 2008). In the age of nationalism, cultures become the natural repositories of political legitimacy (Gellner 1983). Far right-wing parties draw on the ethnic elements of nationalism to gain legitimacy. Ethnic nationalism equates nation and ethnic group and emphasises the need to maintain the nation as an ethnically uniform unit. It is characterised by organic membership and ascriptive criteria of inclusion in the nation, such as blood, creed, and language. The collective is defined in cultural terms as a community of birth, native culture, and common descent (Smith 1991: 20). Most studies of the far right include some analysis of ethnic nationalism, which they consider as a core ideological characteristic of such parties. Far right-wing parties put forward an ethnic understanding of the nation in which non-members are presented as a threat and therefore excluded. This is how they legitimate their anti-EU and anti-immigration stances. In order to understand the success of contemporary far right-wing parties that have distanced themselves from fascism, scholars have also applied the civic framework. Increasingly, radical right-wing parties define 'otherness' in accordance to ideological rather than racial and bloodline criteria (Halikiopoulou et al. 2013). They modernise their ideology by annexing the values of tolerance, liberalism and diversity, thus framing the debate in civic terms.

The ideology of the Golden Dawn may indeed be categorised within the 'ethnic nationalism' variant, emphasising blood, genealogy, and the perennial nature of the Greek nation. However, this ideology goes beyond the ethnic-civic framework in that the party's ultra-nationalism is characterised by a palingenetic vision (Griffin 1991): the need to re-awaken the nation from 'the ashes of an old decadent social order' (Mann 2004: 12). The party adopts an ethnic understanding of the

DOI: 10.1057/9781137535917.0009

Greek nation as defined by ascriptive criteria, having existed since time immemorial, and being inherently superior and heroic in its attempt to put forward its ultra-nationalist palingenetic discourse. Within the same framework, the Golden Dawn utilises 'threats to the nation' as means for mobilising support through a language of chosenness, threat, national defence and national liberation. This forms the party's nationalist solution to the crisis of the nation-state and we conceptualise it in terms of the notions of chosenness and ethnic election that the Golden Dawn put forward in its rhetoric.

The Golden Dawn's palingenetic vision

The Golden Dawn (2012d: 7) sees itself as a crusader with a 'unique mission, because its members do not just belong to any Nation, but rather to the Great Greek Nation which created civilization, which built two world empires and which was reborn like the mythic phoenix from its own ashes with the blood of its Fighters in 1821'. This 'phoenix-like' national rebirth also constitutes the Golden Dawn's vision for contemporary Greece. The party's overall vision is the rebirth of the Greek nation through a populist, purifying, trans-class movement. Nationalism is a 'political, social and ethical revolution, welding the "people" into a dynamic national community under new elites infused with heroic values' (Griffin 1991: xi) and thus forms the justification of the Golden Dawn's fascist ideals, including statism, paramilitarism, transcendence and cleansing. We understand nationalism in this framework as a political religion and examine the Golden Dawn's ideology and discourse through the notions of chosenness and ethnic election. 'Chosenness', or the belief that a certain people or nations are chosen by God, is both missionary and covenantal: missionary because it consists of the belief that the community has been chosen by the deity for a special religious task or mission; and covenantal because it emphasises the idea of a mutual promise, in which a deity choses a community and promises it certain benefits if it in turn obeys the laws and statutes of the deity (Smith 2000).

The Golden Dawn's palingenetic vision is underpinned by a discourse of chosenness. The Greek people are chosen by God. They are a 'super family' (Smith 1992), with a unique culture and a Golden Age to restore. Chosenness entails a parallel with religion: nationalism is not merely an

DOI: 10.1057/9781137535917.0009

ideology, but has a sacred quality. Struggle is also sacred, a moral calling 'to the soul of every Greek who has felt the sacred Duty of the Struggle' (Golden Dawn 09/01/2014) and 'the Duty of our Race' (Golden Dawn 30/10/2013). Salvation too is sacred. The liberation of the nation is a divine calling and a right of birth. The Golden Dawn identifies Greece as a 'chosen land' and itself as having been granted the unique vocation to save the Greek nation from exploitative foreign powers and domestic traitors who have collaborated with them. This will restore Greece to its past greatness as the helm of Western civilisation. 'The Golden Dawn's divine Enlightenment and Struggle will bring about a better future for the Greeks' (Golden Dawn 07/01/2014). The chosen nation is deified and its members have divine and godlike characteristics: 'The Greek soul does not fall apart' (Golden Dawn 04/12/2013); Greeks are 'Titans, Giants and Semi-Gods' (Golden Dawn 25/03/2014); Greekness is organically antithetical to domination (Golden Dawn 19/06/2014) and patriotism is a birth trait. There is an element of ritual and symbolism to this, hence, for example, the importance of the blessing of the revolution and its flag. The party's symbolic colours are black, red and white, 'the colours that Greek independence heroes used in their revolutionary flags' (Golden Dawn 2012d: 10). White resembles the innocence of the struggle against the tyrants; black stands for death for fatherland and freedom; and red for the self-determination of the Greek people. 'Red is the colour of revolution, of blood, of race, the colour of the Spartan robes, the colour of Alexander's [the Great's] flag, the colour of true socialism and social revolution' (Golden Dawn 2012d: 10).

Using Smith's (1999) framework of ethnic election and national destiny, we show how the Golden Dawn presents its palingenetic vision of chosenness in its rhetoric, by focusing on four aspects of ethnic election: the constant reinforcement of a strict boundary between the ethnic community and the other; a sense of moral superiority over outsiders; a doctrine of spiritual liberation that emphasises the community's special destiny and tends to include a radical reversal from its current underdog status; and the necessity of an elite-driven mobilisation. As noted earlier, this goes beyond the framework of ethnic and civic nationalism. Ethnic election is more demanding than ethnocentrism: to be chosen is to be placed under moral obligations (Smith 1992). The link is history: nationalist mobilisation takes place in a historical context, through an attempt to glorify the group's history. 'Experiences of traumatic violence may live on as a part of oral tradition or they may sometimes be perpetuated in

DOI: 10.1057/9781137535917.0009

official history textbooks and public rituals, nourishing calls for revenge; [...] prior exposure to combat means that violence is no longer unthinkable but constitutes part of the accepted repertoire of action' (Cederman et al. 2010: 97).

The Golden Dawn does this by drawing on the available cultural reservoirs in Greece's past. The party emphasises ties with ancient Greece, past wars, imperial experience during the Ottoman years and invasion in the 1940s. In this context, the party makes frequent references to ancient Greece, emphasising the heroic traits of those belonging to the Greek nation. Historical figures, whether heroes of ancient Greece, Byzantium, the Greek War of Independence, the Second World War, or Cyprus are glorified for their heroism, bravery and sacrifice. By referring to a very large array of officially recognised historical events, personalities, and national identity traits and placing them within the ethnic election framework, the Golden Dawn successfully integrates them into its ultra-nationalist palingenetic ideology. The Golden Dawn materials we examine in this chapter provide commentary on a variety of important events in Greek history, as well as some international events, usually on the date of specific anniversary that is a cornerstone event for Greece—for example, 29 May, which is the anniversary of the Sack of Constantinople; 25 March, the anniversary of Greek independence from the Ottoman Empire; and 28 October, which marks the start of Greece's involvement in the Second World War in what is known as the 'epic of the 1940s'. These texts also refer to historical events, which usually involve some reference to prominent Greek writers, artists or politicians, who according to the Golden Dawn's interpretation were sheer nationalists, patriots and anti-communists. These include Kavafis, Palamas, Kazantzakis, Solomos, Mavilis, Myrivilis, and other figures that resonate among the Greek population as distinguished Greeks. The Golden Dawn presents them as figures leading the nationalist cause.

Nationalist mobilisation and ethnic election

The notion of chosenness implies that the nation has a special mission and destiny central to which is its rebirth. The Golden Dawn portrays the Greek nation as *unique* with its individuality, history and destiny and as *superior* because its history and destiny are that of a higher civilisation. The concepts of national mission and national destiny accord nationalism with a religious quality (Smith 1991). They are two different conceptions

DOI: 10.1057/9781137535917.0009

of the collective mission producing similar effects. They both offer 'a common framework of collective meaning' of a unique cultural mission for each people. They share a teleological vision for the collective based on divine right and spiritual salvation. 'This is the linear conception of a community progressing, morally and politically, through time and space, and being required to meet certain conditions and perform certain tasks if it is to find spiritual fulfilment and moral salvation' (Smith 1999: 339). Smith identifies four aspects of ethnic election, which we examine henceforth within the context of the ideology and rhetoric of the Golden Dawn's palingenetic vision.

1 The constant reinforcement of a strict boundary between the ethnic community and the other:

The Golden Dawn cultivates a distinction between ethnic Greeks, who are racially, morally, and culturally superior to other groups, and foreigners, who are both inferior and corrupt. The party presents the Greek nation as a homogenous unit, a community of birth bound by a native culture, organic membership and ascriptive identity traits, including blood, creed and language. These Greek national identity traits are exclusive, organic, and inherited by birth. According to the Golden Dawn the Greek language has survived for 2,800 years (Golden Dawn 25/02/2014). There are frequent references to the Greek 'race', 'Genos' or 'ethnie' denoting the party's understanding of Greek nationalism as a community of common descent, rather than a voluntary union. Greeks are often presented as the chosen people (Smith 2003), historically 'saved by God', bound by their blood, their religion, their language and their 'soul'. The Golden Dawn parallels Greece to a mother 'Hellas', which 'bears children' (Golden Dawn 02/02/2014).

Because the party understands the Greek nation as a natural unit, it repeatedly portrays it as a unified, perennial and un-eroded entity that has existed throughout the *longue durée*. The Golden Dawn's main focus therefore is on the linear progression of the Greek nation through time, ranging from antiquity to modernity. Greek history has ranged from Ancient Sparta, the time of Plato and Homer, the Byzantine Empire and the Greek War of Independence and its heroes (Golden Dawn 2012d: 5). 'We are the descendants of that great Nation, which created Civilisation and of that great thousand year old Empire, which kept the spirit of the East away from Europe until it fell after a heroic struggle, betrayed by the

DOI: 10.1057/9781137535917.0009

West in May 1453' (Golden Dawn 2012d: 6). The party glorifies the past: Greece was 'Great' before and will be again (Golden Dawn 2012d: 7).

The portrayal of the nation as a natural, unified, perennial and un-eroded unit that has existed through time immemorial is at the core of Golden Dawn's ethnocentric claims (Fragoudaki and Dragona 1997: 59). Understanding the Greek nation as an organic entity defined by ethnic identifiers confined to biological and cultural elements explain the Golden Dawn's emphasis on white supremacy. According to the Golden Dawn's own constitution, only those Greeks of Greek blood who have served in the Greek army may become members of the Golden Dawn (*Efimerida ton Sydakton* 2013). The Greek nation is an exclusive club to which membership is restricted. There is a clear line of delineation between members and outsiders. The criteria for inclusion in the Greek nation are ethnic: outsiders are excluded from the national community on the basis of race, creed and ethnicity. Greek status cannot be acquired; it is something one is born into. Racism informs the party policy agenda. The Golden Dawn is staunchly and indiscriminately anti-immigrant, emphasising that there is no such thing as 'legal' immigration. During its electoral campaign in June 2012 many of its members declared that immigration can never be legal; the party manifesto promised that if elected the party would expel all immigrants from Greece. In the same manifesto the party denied the granting of full political rights to any non-Greek—as defined by the biological features described earlier—on the grounds that granting Greek citizenship to non-natives will 'spoil' the continuity of the Greek nation (Golden Dawn 2012d: 5). The organisation of blood donations and 'soup kitchens' intended only for Greeks, a status to be confirmed by the presentation of a Greek identity card to one of the Golden Dawn members on site, also confirms the party's strict boundaries between the Greek ethnic community and others. This is also linked to the party's irredentist policy, which seeks to 'restore' former territories of the Byzantine Empire to the Greek state, including parts of modern Turkey and Cyprus. As such they have also been forging links with the Cypriot far right-wing equivalent party, the National Popular Front (*Εθνικό Λαϊκό Μέτωπο*, ELAM) (Katsourides 2013).

2   A sense of moral superiority over outsiders:

The Golden Dawn attempts to confer on Greek people 'a sense of their moral superiority over outsiders, reinforcing the ethnocentrism which is part and parcel of all ethnic communities' (Smith 1999: 336). The party

DOI: 10.1057/9781137535917.0009

portrays the Greek nation as inherently superior because of ascriptive Greek traits such as bravery, valour, heroism and sacrifice for the nation. The distinguishing feature between 'us' and 'the other' is ethnic superiority based on an idealised vision of Greece and an element of ethnic 'chosenness'. This chosenness stems from Greece's glorious past, the civilisation of the ancient Greek city-states, the legacy of Orthodox Byzantium and its sacred linguistic ethnie. 'Greekness' is presented and perceived in opposition to a hostile 'other'. The narrative stresses the importance of Greek resistance and mobilisation against an 'aggressive enemy' and the achievement of the preservation of Hellenism and all its 'ethnic traits' throughout the centuries. The Golden Dawn focuses on salient historical events, for example, the war of independence, the Greek civil war and the Second World War, which it appropriates within its core ideology and discourse. It is interesting that during the Greek War of Independence, Greece was allegedly not only victimised by the Ottomans, but also the Jews (Golden Dawn 03/01/2014). The Ottoman Empire and modern Turkey are the 'perennial enemy of the Genos' (Golden Dawn 05/01/2014), simultaneously inferior, hostile and irredentist (Golden Dawn 28/05/2014).

This encompasses the Golden Dawn's sense of Greek superiority over all 'others' who are portrayed as 'barbarians' (Golden Dawn 19/06/2014). 'No Race, no Nation has ever offered what the Greek race has offered' (Golden Dawn 28/05/2014). Greeks are distinguished because of their dignity, pride and honour. They may 'have endured a lot, but their Dignity, Pride, and Honour are superior to all' (Golden Dawn 20/11/2013a). Greeks have ideals and a moral right to fight others for these ideals: 'the genuine Greek ideal is faith in Motherland and religion (Golden Dawn 19/11/2013). 'It is our sacred duty' to 'enclose within our soul these immortal ideals' (Golden Dawn 19/11/2013). Greeks will fight to the death and not surrender. This moral ideal is ingrained in the Greek psyche, it is an innate attribute with which Greeks are born. This theme characterises Greeks from antiquity. Golden Dawn materials are replete with references to Greek historical figures and events, from the time of ancient Greece till the contemporary era, glorified for their bravery, heroism and sacrifice for the Greek nation. Famous figures are referenced, ranging from Achilles, who 'was more afraid of living in disgrace' (Golden Dawn 30/05/2014), to 'the heroic struggles of the Macedons whose unbeatable mental strength constitutes yet another glorious chapter in the History of the Greek Nation' (Golden Dawn 13/10/2013), to 'the proud NO that

DOI: 10.1057/9781137535917.0009

shook humanity!' (Golden Dawn 28/10/2013). The party here refers to Ioannis Metaxas's refusal to co-operate with the axis powers, which signalled the invasion of Greece in 1940. The Golden Dawn also has a sub-section in its website under the title 'Unknown figures of Hellenism', which posts biographies of historical figures, who the Golden Dawn deems heroic but are less famous. In forging these historical links, the Golden Dawn attempts to confer on the members of the Greek nation a sense of their own superiority against outsiders.

3   A doctrine of spiritual liberation that emphasises the community's special destiny and tends to include a radical reversal from its current underdog status:

The Golden Dawn links the superiority of the Greek nation to the idea of Greece's 'special destiny', which is bound to 'see a radical reversal of its hitherto lowly or marginal status in the world. This is a doctrine of spiritual liberation, which asserts that virtue will be rewarded in the latter days, when the last shall be first—and it applies with special force in the case of covenantal myths' (Smith 1999: 336). The Golden Dawn's palingenetic vision is linked to a form of nationalism that offers a scheme of status reversal. The party portrays the Greek nation as great and as having been wronged by external powers. The primary goal is the restoration of this past glory. The discourse of the Golden Dawn tends to be underpinned by a language of liberation, restoration of national sovereignty, resistance to foreign domination and struggle against external impositions. The Greeks are special; they fight with 'heroism and a holy mania' (Golden Dawn 25/09/2013) and will restore the nation's former glory with their heroism and self-sacrifice. The importance of the concept of 'sacrificial death' is a central component of the collective power of nationalism (Marvin and Ingle 1998). Hence, the Golden Dawn portrays sacrifice as not only desirable, but also essential to the ultimate goal of palingenesis, 'which requires plenty of Greek blood' (Golden Dawn 09/04/2014). The party glorifies the act of sacrifice for the collective good of the nation; giving up one's life for the survival of the group is the ultimate collective sacrifice. All members of the group, precisely in order to be members of the group, have to identify with this sacrifice or the symbol of the sacrifice. This has parallels with religion: those who die for the nation are ethnomartyrs or 'the neomartyrs of the Genos' (Golden Dawn 08/04/2014). These ethnomartyrs are in peace, having chosen the path 'of sacrifice and glory' (Golden Dawn 14/03/2014). 'The shrines of

DOI: 10.1057/9781137535917.0009

the Genos, the legends of the Motherland are enriched with yet another Hero' (Golden Dawn 14/03/2014). The duty to honour 'the heroes who fought and sacrificed their lived for the grandeur of our nation' is sacred (Golden Dawn 06/04/2014). Their struggle is also God-given and has been there since time immemorial: this allows the Golden Dawn to use all past battles, wars and struggles, pointing to the heroism of the Greeks throughout the longue durée. These include, among numerous examples, Alexander the Great (e.g., Golden Dawn 25/11/2013), the battle of Marathon (e.g., Golden Dawn 12/11/2013), the battle of Crete (Golden Dawn 09/11/2013), and the epic of the 1940s in Korytsa (e.g., Golden Dawn 22/11/2013).

Commemorating the war dead embeds these triumphs and disasters within the ideal of self-sacrifice in order to achieve eternity of the nation which is 'why military heroes and battles are such an important part of the nationalist narrative' (Kaldor 2004: 165). The Golden Dawn has devised the concept of the 'pantheon of heroes', which features prominently in its website. Through this concept, the party grants a religious quality to all Greeks whose death is somehow associated with the nation. It appropriates well-known Greek heroes in this rhetoric; figures who the official state recognises as Greek heroes, portrayed as such in national historiography, school text books and national museums. There, in the 'pantheon of heroes' rest the heroic souls of Greeks including 'Achilles, Leonidas, Alexander the Great, Basil the Bulgar-slayer, Constantine Palaiologos, Theodoros Kolokotronis, Nikitaras the Turk-eater, Karaiskakis, Pavlos Melas, Grigorios Afxentiou, Georgios Grivas' (Golden Dawn 13/05/2014). These prominent Greeks fulfilled Greece's special destiny in the past by liberating it from its oppressors and by restoring Greece's greatness. The pantheon of heroes is thus a key rhetorical strategy in the Golden Dawn's palingenetic discourse.

4   The necessity of an elite-driven mobilisation:

Finally, the Golden Dawn presents itself as the necessary leader who will 'tap the energies that lie within' (Smith 1999: 336) and fight for national rebirth, speaking in the name of whole people. The party sees itself as a movement from below which embodies the collective will of the Greek people and the epitome of the Greek nation. The restoration of Greece's past glory can only be initiated by authentic nationalists, none other than the Golden Dawn, who will purify the nation from the anti-nationalist elements that are responsible for its demise. The party therefore has a

DOI: 10.1057/9781137535917.0009

'calling' to save the Greek nation from exploitative foreigners and domestic traitors who have collaborated with them and thus restore Greece to its past greatness as the helm of Western civilisation.

The nation is perpetually under threat by those not belonging to the ethnic community and their corrupt domestic collaborators who serve the interests of foreign powers. These constitute 'dark, despotic forces set against Hellenism' (Golden Dawn 27/05/2014). The party's vocation is to salvage the nation. 'We, the Greek nationalists swear to restore the Truth and to educate the future generations of Greeks with a slogan that will be engraved in their hearts: The Blood that flows seeks revenge' (Golden Dawn 23/05/2014). This has allowed the Golden Dawn to link its rhetoric with the crisis. The party has a duty to resurrect the 'weary Greek Genos' (Golden Dawn 17/03/2014), which has suffered from moral, economic, political and social decay. 'Divine enlightenment and the Golden Dawn's Struggle will bring a better future to the Greeks' (Golden Dawn 07/01/2014). By presenting Europe as a problem of national exploitation, the party focuses on national sovereignty as the key issue. It draws parallels with Greece's historical battles for the restoration of national sovereignty, for instance against the Ottoman Empire in the 19th century and Nazi Germany in the 1940s. The rhetoric is one that emphasises the distinction between superior and inferior nations, the strong sense of Greek ethnic superiority and the portrayal of the Greek nation under threat. 'The struggle will be tough, but we Greeks as the worthy followers of our semi-god ancestors will fight and will not cease fighting until we have Won' (Golden Dawn 30/10/2013). The ultimate 'calling' of the 'chosen' nation is its rebirth and this can only be initiated by the nationalists.

> Greek Popular Nationalism has a sacred duty to deliver Greece un-eroded to the next Generation. The generation that will forget will be the last. Our popular tradition lies both in darkness and in light through the passing of time. It lies in darkness for the barbarians. And it lies in darkness for the profane. It is however bright for our followers. (Golden Dawn 12/11/2013)

Conclusion

In this chapter we have placed Golden Dawn's ideology within the framework of palingenetic ultra-nationalism, 'namely the myth that the organically conceived nation is to be cleansed of decadence and

DOI: 10.1057/9781137535917.0009

comprehensively renewed' (Griffin 2004: 299). The party's palingenetic vision is underpinned by a discourse of chosenness and ethnic election. The Golden Dawn portrays Greeks as a people chosen by God. As such, restoration of past glory is presented as a right of birth and is at the core of the party's palingenetic appeal. Greeks are distinct from all outsiders, they are superior to all outsiders, they have a special destiny to lead Western civilisation and only the Golden Dawn can lead them to fulfil their destiny. This is the Golden Dawn's special calling.

Together with the twin fascist myth of social decadence, examined in the previous chapter, this constitutes the Golden Dawn's nationalist solution to the Greek crisis. This solution promises an escape from the current decadent system and all its ills by proposing an alternative path for Greece. In this alternative path, Greece's past glory has been formally restored by a popular movement from below, embodied by the Golden Dawn and its leader. Only Greek nationalists inhabit this alternative ideal Greece. There are no longer any societal divisions, as these have been transcended and substituted by the singular will of the people. Internal and external enemies have been cleansed, and the nation has been purified. In this society there is no atomisation and no individual outside nationalism. The nation has been reborn from its ashes and has reached the Promised Land, where there is no disillusionment, no dissatisfaction, no crisis, no corruption, and no societal decay.

DOI: 10.1057/9781137535917.0009

6
Conclusion

Abstract: *The aim of this chapter is twofold. First, it summarises the main arguments and findings of the book, focusing on demand- and supply-side dynamics. More specifically, the chapter discusses the ways in which the Golden Dawn has capitalised on social discontent by putting forward its 'nationalist solution', that is, a discourse, which emphasises the twin fascist myths of societal decline and national rebirth. Second, the chapter places the Golden Dawn within the broader framework of democratic politics and Greek political culture, discussing the potential implications of this phenomenon on policy and the political mainstream.*

Keywords: argument summary; Greek political culture; policy implications

Vasilopoulou, Sofia and Daphne Halikiopoulou. *The Golden Dawn's 'Nationalist Solution': Explaining the Rise of the Far Right in Greece*. New York: Palgrave Macmillan, 2015. DOI: 10.1057/9781137535917.0010.

DOI: 10.1057/9781137535917.0010

The rise of the Golden Dawn: disillusionment, social decadence and national rebirth

In June 2012 over 400,000 Greek citizens voted for the Golden Dawn, a far right-wing party with a fascist ideology, granting it 18 seats in a parliament of 300. How can a country which experienced a military dictatorship only a few decades before and which fought Nazism only a few years earlier grant parliamentary representation and endorse the practices of such a group? A potential answer is economic crisis, the same answer that was offered as a framework for understanding the rise of fascism and Nazism in inter-war Europe. However, a brief comparative outlook shows the limitations of such an explanation. First, Spain and Portugal, which both experienced the severity of the Eurozone crisis and in addition share with Greece the historical experience of military dictatorship, did not experience a rise of the far right. On the contrary, parties with a similar ideology to the Golden Dawn including the Spanish España 2000, National Democracy and the Portuguese Partido Nacional Renovador (PNR) remained marginalised both in the 2011 national elections in the two countries, as well as the 2014 European Parliament elections. Second, European countries that did not experience comparable economic crisis conditions did witness the rise of far right-wing parties, including, for example, the United Kingdom, Finland, Sweden, France and Austria during the 2014 European Parliament elections. Unlike in Greece, the successful far right-wing parties in these Western European countries maybe categorised within the radical right variety of the far right, having openly attempted to distance themselves from fascism.

Why has economic crisis become associated with the rise of right-wing extremism in Greece but not in other countries that have experienced severe economic crisis? And how may we explain the rise of a far right-wing party with a fascist ideology, which counters the general European trend? This book has attempted to understand the rise of the Golden Dawn within the context of the Greek crisis. It has assessed both demand- and supply-side dynamics, pointing to their interdependence. In particular, this book has shown that the rise of the Golden Dawn in Greece has been the product of three simultaneous conditions: an overall crisis of the nation-state and democracy, giving rise to high levels of political disillusionment and presenting a small far right-wing party with an opportunity to shape its own demand through articulating a 'nationalist' solution to the crisis.

DOI: 10.1057/9781137535917.0010

Greece differs from other European countries that faced economic malaise, not simply in the extent of the economic crisis, but rather the *nature* of the crisis it experienced. This crisis affected society well beyond the economic sphere because of its significant political and ideological dimensions. While the crisis in Spain and Portugal, for example, resulted mainly in the punishment of the incumbent, in Greece it shook the foundations of the system itself. The crisis served as a shock revealing the systemic weaknesses of Greece's clientelism and de-legitimised the main actors in the political system. By challenging the system at its core, the crisis revealed the weak foundations of Greek institutions. It was a crisis of democracy and a crisis of the nation-state, questioning the very legitimacy of the social contract that binds the nation and the state together.

This observation regarding the nature of the Greek crisis has pointed us towards Mann's (2004) explanation for the rise of fascism. We have proposed an explanation, which understands the Golden Dawn as a fascist party and the conditions that gave rise to it as different from the conditions that facilitate the rise of the radical right-wing parties of the West. While various theories seek to explain the phenomenon of fascism, either in terms of class (Lipset 1960) or in terms of ideology (Griffin 1991), Mann's (2004: 365) explanation starts from the premise of the four sources of social power and argues that 'fascists were generated in large numbers by postwar crises in ideological, economic, military, and political power relations to which a transcendent nation-statist ideology spearheaded by "popular" paramilitaries offered a plausible solution'. While we identify three sets of crises in Greece—economic, political and ideological—as opposed to Mann's four, that is, economic, political, ideological, and military, we understand the rise of the Golden Dawn similarly to Mann as a response to an overall crisis of the nation-state and democratic politics.

Within the context of this all-encompassing crisis, political disillusionment in Greece became widespread, cutting across objective socio-economic lines. This theoretical framework works well with our findings from the quantitative analysis that socio-economic characteristics, and more specifically class, are not necessarily good predictors of Golden Dawn support. Instead, the broad electoral base of the Golden Dawn and the power of political attitudes that cut across class lines point us to the relevance of supply. In particular we have examined this in terms of the Golden Dawn's nationalist response to the crisis, with reference

DOI: 10.1057/9781137535917.0010

to Griffin's (1991) twin fascist myths of social decadence and national rebirth. Our analysis indicates that the Golden Dawn's nationalist solution found resonance mainly among disillusioned voters with right-wing ideas.

This manuscript addresses a timely question with comparative significance. The fact that in Western Europe only Greece has experienced the rise of the fascist variety of the far right points to the importance of distinguishing between the different types of far right-wing parties that may enjoy success in contemporary Europe. It also points to the importance of unpacking the concept of crisis and its consequences, distinguishing crises not only in terms of their economic severity, but also their systemic implications. It is limited to assume that economic crisis conditions will automatically lead to the rise of the far right. What we have attempted to clarify in this manuscript is how specific conditions regarding the nature of the crisis and the type of far right-wing party facilitated the rise of the Greek Golden Dawn.

Greek nationalist political culture

An examination of the rise of far right-wing parties also requires a focus on the cultural context within which these parties operate. Overall, a party is more likely to increase its support when some of the values it puts forward are at least not alien to the dominant nationalist culture. Because of its traditionalist orientation and emphasis on defiance, resistance and the ultimate value of national self-determination for the homogenous and organically defined Greek nation, Greek nationalism contains elements that are not antithetical to the ideology of far right-wing parties. As such, it may provide cultural opportunities for parties such as the Golden Dawn, especially at times of crisis when nationalism tends to intensify (Brubaker 2011: 94).

In Greece a predominantly ethnic variant of nationalism constitutes mainstream political culture and is upheld, albeit to different extents, by all political forces regardless of ideology or other social cleavages. Greek society is polarised along the lines of a left-right cleavage but united by nationalism (Kalyvas and Marantzidis 2002; Halikiopoulou et al. 2012). The process of democratic consolidation during the post-dictatorship era was able to contain but not eradicate nationalism, and especially its exclusionary, xenophobic character (Fragoudaki 2013). While Greece

DOI: 10.1057/9781137535917.0010

maintained a democratic institutional system following the restoration of democracy in 1974, it did not progress beyond entrenched and rent-seeking clientelistic networks (Pappas 2013). Especially since the election of PASOK in 1981, the democratic system became premised on populism, that is, the consolidation of mainstream parties not based on liberal terms and strong democratic institutions, but rather on patronage and a bi-polar logic of 'us' the people against the 'exploitative' establishment (Pappas 2013). This system 'allowed Greece to develop politically and economically during periods of international financial stability, but at the same time has rendered the country unable to withstand external shocks' (Vasilopoulou et al. 2014). The shock brought about by the Greek crisis opened up cultural opportunities.

Many of the ideas of the Golden Dawn appear at least consistent with—albeit an extreme version of—the dominant narrative of Greek nationalism. The ideology of the Golden Dawn emphasises the need to maintain the nation as a homogenous unit. This is in line with Greece's version of nationalism, which tends to be understood as ethnic and/or genealogical, defined by an emphasis on a community of birth and native culture, organic membership and ascriptive criteria of inclusion in the nation, including blood, creed and language (Smith 1991). The emphasis on homogeneity and ethnic superiority premised on genealogy fosters a sentiment of exclusion and promotes intolerance (Fragoudaki 2013). This has provided the Golden Dawn with increased opportunities to present immigration as a question of welfare, that is, who should be entitled to the collective goods of the state, in a country where because of the severe crisis the collective goods of the state were scarce. This allowed the party to link its nationalist narrative, that is, who may be understood as belonging to the Greek nation, with economic narratives, for example, welfare provision, scarcity of resources and sovereignty over economic decision-making.

The Golden Dawn's emphasis on resistance, defiance and anomie are also consistent with Greece's official version of nationalism. Resistance and defiance are directed to those outsiders that seem to undermine the sovereignty of the Greek nation. Certain authoritarian values, such as violence, punishment and the establishment of a particular order, are acceptable as long as they promote the non-negotiable homogeneity of the Greek nation. In addition, the ideals, symbols and heroes of Greek nationalism are rarely associated with democratic or moderate ideas. They tend to emphasise valour, justify hatred, anomie (Psychogios 2013)

DOI: 10.1057/9781137535917.0010

and a divine duty to physically eliminate enemies and the necessity of sacrifice (Fragoudaki 2013).

Also consistent with Golden Dawn ideals is the dichotomy ingrained within Greek nationalism between superior and inferior nations. This is reflected in Greek education textbooks, which deny the influences of other civilisations on the Greek because that would make Greece appear inferior (Fragoudaki 2013). The dominant narrative that emphasises Greece's glorious past and its sacred linguistic ethnie (Smith 2003) was institutionalised during the post-independence period by formal state means such as the education system where the Greek nation is portrayed as un-altered since antiquity. Greek collective memory emphasises the superiority of Greek Orthodox descent, Greece's unique language and ancient heritage and the glorification of struggle against the other, which tends to be aggressive and expansionist but culturally inferior (Smith 2003; Fragoudaki and Dragona 1997; Koulouri 2002). Thus the official means of the dissemination and maintenance of Greek national identity tend to promote xenophobia and the sense of a threatened identity (Fragoudaki 1997: 143). This interacts with a political 'culture of sympathy' to acts of resistance against the state (Andronikidou and Kovras 2012). Greece lacks a culture of tolerance: that is, the recognition of groups with whom one disagrees to freely express their opinion and compete for power.

Policy implications and the future of democratic politics in Greece

The rise of the Golden Dawn and its popular endorsement in the Greek political system raises a number of questions regarding the nature of democratic politics. The ability of the Golden Dawn to function within the confines of parliamentary rule shifted certain debates—and by exten-sion the policy agenda—in Greece on a number of issues and had signifi-cant policy implications with regard to issues of toleration, immigration, violence, and law and order. In a country where ethnic nationalism prevails and religion is hardly decoupled from politics, the boundaries of toleration are precarious (Halikiopoulou 2011). The progressive entrenchment of the Golden Dawn has revealed the weak foundations of tolerance and pluralism in Greece, pushing those boundaries further. The various events that took place after Golden Dawn's election in 2012

DOI: 10.1057/9781137535917.0010

revealed the degree to which the party was able to manipulate these boundaries.

Intolerance is a mix of religious and nationalist ideals with significant implications for freedom of speech and acceptance of minority views. The example of the treatment of the Greek version of Terrence McNally's *Corpus Christi* illustrates the extent to which this intolerance may become banal: a part of everyday life, a widely accepted master narrative, an almost self-concealing form of intolerance. *Corpus Christi* is a Passion play that tells the story of Christ and the Apostles, whom it portrays as homosexuals. The play was first staged in New York in the late 1990s and received a mixed reception because of its controversial message. Terrence McNally received various death threats since the opening of the play in the United States. In October 1999, after the play's staging in London, McNally received a death fatwa by a UK-based Islamic group. Thirteen years later, the play stirred a similar controversy in Greece when a Greek theatre company prepared to stage its premiere at a small theatre in central Athens. But this time, protest did not stem only from marginalised fundamentalist groups, but also from ordinary Greek citizens, as well as some clerics belonging to the established Greek Orthodox Church, and some Golden Dawn members and MPs. Many Orthodox Christians protested outside the theatre, registering their objection to the play's moral agenda. This belief, some protesters sought to express not through peaceful demonstrating, but through imposition of violence and verbal abuse. These were notably Golden Dawn members and MPs who also issued threats to the actors and their families. According to them, anyone who claims their right to choose their sexual orientation, who may espouse a religion different to Orthodoxy, or indeed no religion at all, and who may be of different ethnicity does not belong to the Greek nation. They objected to the play on the basis that it is blasphemous and counters the religious consciousness of the overwhelming majority of the Greek people. The premiere was cancelled, and the play was eventually withdrawn.

Although it was the Golden Dawn that radicalised the protest against *Corpus Christi*, all protest stemmed from an ethno-religious objection against the moral message of the play. This argumentation shared a number of common features: a moral conservatism; an intolerance towards minorities whether they be religious, ethnic or social; and a justification of this position on the basis of defending Greek national identity. Steven Billington, the actor who portrayed Judas during the

DOI: 10.1057/9781137535917.0010

London staging of the play back in 1999, argued that *Corpus Christi* is 'a very important play with a message about tolerance' (BBC 1999). The events that unfolded outside the Hytirio theatre in Athens over a decade later, revealed the extent to which intolerance, in terms of religious pluralism, freedom of speech and the acceptance of minority views underpins Greek society. This intolerance is an amalgamation of religious and nationalist ideals. What was at stake during the Hytirio protests was not simply the moral message of the play; it was the broader issue of the acceptance of the rights of others to hold beliefs that one may disagree with.

The Hytirio incident was not an isolated one. In September 2012, a 27-year-old Greek was arrested for 'malicious blasphemy' and 'religious offence'. His 'crime' was to publish satirical comments about a Greek Holy Man, Elder Paisios, on Facebook. The indictment was prompted by the numerous complaints put forward by various Christian groups and individual citizens as early as July 2012 (*Ta Nea* 2012). The arrest took place a few days after Christos Pappas, Golden Dawn MP, made a motion in the Greek parliament on the issue. However, Greek police denied a direct link between the motion and the arrest, arguing that the operation to intervene had commenced prior to Mr. Pappas's motion. Regardless of whether the Golden Dawn played a part in instigating the arrest, the issue is really about freedom of speech and toleration.

The Greek government during this period attempted to address the issue of the rise of extremism, but often this entailed shifting the policy agenda to more conservative and stricter laws, for example, tightening immigration and citizenship. Partly, this was a response to the rising anti-immigration sentiments capitalised on by the neo-Nazi Golden Dawn which targeted all foreigners on the basis of belonging to a different ethnicity and a different 'infidel' religion. The introduction of the 'Ξένιος Ζευς' or 'Hospitable Zeus' policy in 2012 aimed at decreasing the numbers of illegal immigrants in Greece, which were estimated as very high, by securing Greek borders and deporting those with no legal right to remain in the country. The implementation of this policy was characterised by an overt discrimination, racism on both ethnic and religious grounds and human rights abuse. According to *Kathimerini* (2013), in February 2013 and so six months after the introduction of this policy, while 77,526 people had been detained, only 4,435 were arrested on the grounds of illegal stay. Therefore, a mere 5.7 per cent were detained on the basis of actually being illegal. Those detained tended to be people

DOI: 10.1057/9781137535917.0010

who do not visually resemble Greek ethnic background (e.g., in terms of racial origin and religious clothing). Within this process, tourists visiting the country on vacation were also targeted, sometimes assaulted on racist grounds (BBC 2013). These practices were condemned by various human rights organisations, including Human Rights Watch which published a 52-page report entitled 'Unwelcome guests: Greek police abuses of migrants in Athens'. According to the author of the report, Eva Cossé, immigrants 'are regularly stopped, searched and detained just because of the way they look' (Human Rights Watch 2013). The problematic implementation of an already sensitive and to an extent discriminatory policy such as 'Hospitable Zeus' served to legitimise hatred against ethnic and religious minorities. Cases of racist violence increased in Greece at that time—often occurring outside unofficial places of worship for the non-Orthodox.

Three points are particularly interesting regarding these developments. First, the deeply intolerant message directed against a number of groups, including homosexuals, people with left-leaning attitudes, members of other religions, and foreigners; second, the support for the message of intolerance by some Greek Orthodox Church clerics; and third, the inability or unwillingness of the police to intervene, alluding to potential links between the Golden Dawn and the Greek Police Force. If we understand the police force in Weberian terms, that is, as a body that exercises legitimate violence on behalf of the state, then the potential link between the Golden Dawn and the Greek Police Force has significant implications for the nature and future of Greek democracy.

The ability of the Golden Dawn to operate within the confines of parliamentary politics significantly impacted on Greek society, both directly and indirectly. Beyond shifting the policy agenda and legitimising exclusionary and conservative policies, it also revealed the deeply ingrained intolerance and propensity towards violence especially in a society ridden by crisis. One of the potential remedies for the Golden Dawn phenomenon discussed in Greece included the constitutional outlawing of the party especially after the arrest of its MPs. However, the danger of such a solution may be that it is at best temporary and at worse could have the reverse effect of increasing the party's support. A longer standing solution should include longer-term policies leading towards the cultivation of a more tolerant political culture that accepts the rights of groups with whom one disagrees to freely and peacefully

DOI: 10.1057/9781137535917.0010

express their opinion and compete for power. This can only be facilitated by educational reform and civic engagement.

Broader relevance and avenues for future research

In this book we have provided a detailed analysis of the rise of the Golden Dawn in the context of the Greek crisis. Our analysis opens up avenues for future research, both in terms of Greek domestic politics and in terms of the broader applicability of our argument. With regard to the Golden Dawn itself, we only had a limited period during which the party enjoyed parliamentary representation in order to analyse its ideology, discourse and programmatic agenda. Further research examining a longer period of time would systematise the changes that the party underwent after its entry in the Greek Parliament. It is also important to examine the extent to which the Golden Dawn compares to other parties on the right of the political spectrum in Greece and to systematise its effects on party competition since 2012. Has the party's entry in the system influenced the policy agenda of other parties? Finally, further research could shed light on the broader question of social cleavages: Has the success of the Golden Dawn given rise to new dimensions of conflict in Greece, such as a cultural dimension, and has this affected the importance of the traditional left-right cleavage?

With regard to the broader applicability of our arguments, further research could examine the rise of the Golden Dawn comparatively, systematising the two points that have been raised in this book but not analysed in depth. First, why did the rise of the far right take place in Greece but not in other countries that experienced comparable economic crisis; and second, how does the rise of the Golden Dawn compare to the rise of other far right-wing parties in Western Europe where the general trend is a disassociation from fascism and overt violence? If our analysis is correct, Spain and Portugal have not experienced the rise of a party similar to the Golden Dawn because of the nature of the crisis that they faced. The same may apply to Ireland. In addition, the conditions that give rise to radical right-wing parties in Western Europe may be different from those that facilitated the rise of the Golden Dawn. A systematic comparison of demand- and supply-side dynamics across Europe would shed light on the different patterns that exist in each set of cases. Cyprus could be a particularly interesting case for comparison as

DOI: 10.1057/9781137535917.0010

it shares common history and political culture with Greece and, the far right-wing ELAM puts forward a highly nationalistic agenda. Further research could also systematise the similarities and differences between Western and Eastern European far right-wing parties. For example, the Hungarian Jobbik is in many ways similar to the Golden Dawn; yet Hungary's communist past, and in many ways different political system, could point to a different pattern among post-communist countries.

Finally, it is important to examine the broader implications of this phenomenon for the nature and scope of contemporary European democracy and policy outcomes. The rise of far right-wing parties, their endorsement and consolidation in the system raises the issue of the radicalisation of the mainstream related to areas such as censorship and freedom of speech, as well as mainstream party response towards these sensitive policy debates. For example, the adoption of stricter immigration policies, the outlawing of specific backlash extremist groups, the issue of legality, the question of impunity of MPs and the longer-term policy solutions for countering support such as educational reform and means of fostering civic engagement. To what extent does entering electoral politics entail the legitimisation of violence and as such the 'radicalisation' of the political system as a whole? Or conversely, does entering the democratic process imply the mainstreaming of such movements, the abandonment of violence and the modernisation of their ideas? How can we strengthen democracy and reverse this phenomenon, for example, through educational reform and the promotion of formal civil society institutions? How may we channel disillusionment through the means of democratic participation especially within the current context of economic crisis and severe austerity, which have created a platform for anti-politics?

DOI: 10.1057/9781137535917.0010

Appendix

TABLE A.1   *Overlap in PTVs of Golden Dawn and other Greek parties*

		ANEL			
		$0 \le x \le 3$ (%)	$4 \le x \le 6$ (%)	$7 \le x \le 10$ (%)	Total (%)
Golden Dawn	$0 \le x \le 3$	86.80	7.20	6.00	100
	$4 \le x \le 6$	53.40	32.90	13.70	100
	$7 \le x \le 10$	77.80	7.90	14.30	100
	Total	84.10	8.60	7.20	100

N = 1330; gamma = 0.424, p-value<.01

		New Democracy			
		$0 \le x \le 3$ (%)	$4 \le x \le 6$ (%)	$7 \le x \le 10$ (%)	Total (%)
Golden Dawn	$0 \le x \le 3$	69.10	9.40	21.50	100
	$4 \le x \le 6$	67.10	11.00	21.90	100
	$7 \le x \le 10$	72.40	6.30	21.30	100
	Total	69.40	9.20	21.50	100

N = 1341, gamma = −0.026, p-value>.10

		Olive Tree			
		$0 \le x \le 3$ (%)	$4 \le x \le 6$ (%)	$7 \le x \le 10$ (%)	Total (%)
Golden Dawn	$0 \le x \le 3$	79.30	8.50	12.30	100
	$4 \le x \le 6$	93.70	4.80	1.60	100
	$7 \le x \le 10$	98.40		1.60	100
	Total	81.70	7.50	10.80	100

N = 1320; gamma = −0.764, p-value<.01

		DIMAR			
		$0 \le x \le 3$ (%)	$4 \le x \le 6$ (%)	$7 \le x \le 10$ (%)	Total (%)
Golden Dawn	$0 \le x \le 3$	75.30	15.40	9.30	100
	$4 \le x \le 6$	94.40	4.20	1.40	100
	$7 \le x \le 10$	94.40	1.60	4.00	100
	Total	78.10	13.50	8.40	100

N = 1338; gamma = −0.657, p-value<.01

		SYRIZA			
		$0 \le x \le 3$ (%)	$4 \le x \le 6$ (%)	$7 \le x \le 10$ (%)	Total (%)
Golden Dawn	$0 \le x \le 3$	58.40	10.40	31.30	100
	$4 \le x \le 6$	53.50	5.60	40.80	100
	$7 \le x \le 10$	60.30	22.20	17.50	100
	Total	58.30	11.20	30.50	100

N = 1326; gamma = −0.042, p-value>.10

		KKE			
		$0 \le x \le 3$ (%)	$4 \le x \le 6$ (%)	$7 \le x \le 10$ (%)	Total (%)
Golden Dawn	$0 \le x \le 3$	77.70	9.70	12.50	100
	$4 \le x \le 6$	76.90	9.20	13.80	100
	$7 \le x \le 10$	84.80	7.20	8.00	100
	Total	78.30	9.50	12.20	100

N = 1330; gamma = −0.133; p-value>.10

DOI: 10.1057/9781137535917.0011

References

Adorno, T.W., Frenkel-Brunswik, E., Levinson, D.J. and
Sanford, B. (1969) *The Authoritarian Personality.* New
York: W.W. Norton.

Andreadis, I. (2014) Weights for the Hellenic Panel
Study of EES 2014. Ann Arbor, MI: Inter-university
Consortium for Political; Social Research [distributor].
doi:10.3886/E12611V1, available at: http://dx.doi.
org/10.3886/E12611V1.

Andreadis, I., Schmitt, H., Teperoglou, E. and
Chadjipadelis, T. (2014) Hellenic Panel Study:
European Election Study. Ann Arbor, MI: Inter-
university Consortium for Political and Social
Research [distributor], 2014–08-24, available at: http://
doi.org/10.3886/E11431V12.

Andronikidou, A. and Kovras, I. (2012) 'Cultures of
rioting and anti-systemic politics in Southern Europe',
West European Politics, 35(4): 707–725.

Arendt, H. (1951) *The Origins of Totalitarianism.* Cleveland,
OH: Meridian Books.

BBC (1999) 'UK Fatwa for "gay Jesus" writer'. 29
October, available at: http://news.bbc.co.uk/2/hi/
uk_news/493436.stm.

——— (2013) 'The tourists held by Greek police as illegal
migrants'. 10 January, available at: http://www.bbc.
co.uk/news/magazine-20958353.

Bell, D. (1964) 'The dispossessed', in Bell, D. (ed.) *The
Radical Right.* Garden City, NY: Anchor, pp. 1–45.

Betz, H.-G. (1993) 'The new politics of resentment: Radical right-wing populist parties in Western Europe', *Comparative Politics*, 25(4): 413–427.

—— (1994) *Radical Right-Wing Populism in Western Europe*. Houndmills: Macmillan.

—— (1998) 'Introduction', in Betz, H.-G. and Immerfall, S. (eds.) *The New Politics of the Right: Neo-populist Parties and Movements in Established Democracies*. New York: St. Martin's.

Bitsika, P. (2010) 'Η Βαβέλ της Αριστεράς' (The babel of the left), Ta Nea, 20 June, available at: http://www.tovima.gr/politics/article/?aid√4338701.

Bochsler, D. and Sciarini, P. (2010) 'So close but so far: Voting propensity and party choice for left-wing parties', *Swiss Political Science Review*, 16(3): 373–402.

Breuilly, J. (1993) *Nationalism and the State*. Manchester: Manchester University Press.

Brown, D. (1999) 'Are there good and bad nationalisms?', *Nations and Nationalism*, 5(2): 281–302.

Brubaker, R. (2003) 'The Manichean myth: Rethinking the distinction between 'civic' and 'ethnic' nationalism', in Kriesi, H., Armigeon, K., Slegrist, H. and Wimmer, A. (eds.) *Nation and National Identity: The European Experience in Perspective*. West Lafayette: Purdue University Press.

—— (2011) 'Economic crisis, nationalism and politicised ethnicity', in Calhoun, C. and Derluguian G. (eds.) *The Deepening Crisis: Governance Challenges after Neoliberalism*. New York: New York University Press.

Calhoun, C. (2007) *Nations Matter: Culture, History and the Cosmopolitan Dream*. London and New York: Routledge.

Carsten, F. (1980) *The Rise of Fascism*. Berkeley and Los Angeles: University of California Press.

Carter, E. (2002) 'Proportional representation and the fortunes of right-wing extremist parties', *West European Politics*, 25(3): 125–146.

—— (2005) *The Extreme Right in Western Europe: Success or Failure?* Manchester: Manchester University Press.

Cederman, L., Wimmer, A. and Min, B. (2010) 'Why do ethnic groups rebel? New data and analysis', *World Politics*, 62(1): 87–119.

Chhibber, P. and Torcal, M. (1997) 'Elite strategy, social cleavages, and party systems in a new democracy: Spain', *Comparative Political Studies*, 1(30): 27–54.

DOI: 10.1057/9781137535917.0012

Cutts, D., Ford, R. and Goodwin, M. (2011) 'Anti-immigrant, politically disaffected or still racist after all? Examining the attitudinal drivers of extreme right support in Britain in the 2009 European elections', *European Journal of Political Research*, 50: 418–440.

Dinas, E., Georgiadou, V., Konstantinidis, I. and Rori, L. (2015 forthcoming) 'From dusk to dawn: Local party organization and party success of right-wing extremism', *Party Politics*, doi: 10.1177/1354068813511381.

Eatwell, R. (1996) 'On defining the fascist minimum: The centrality of ideology', *Journal of Political Ideologies*, 1(3): 303–319.

———— (2000) 'The rebirth of the extreme right in Western Europe?', *Parliamentary Affairs*, 53(3): 407–425.

———— (2001) 'Universal fascism? Approaches and definitions', in S.U. Larsen (ed.) *Fascism outside Europe*. New York: Columbia University Press.

———— (2005) 'Charisma and the revival of the European extreme right', in Rydgren, J. (ed.) *Movements of Exclusion: Radical Right-Wing Populism in the Western World*. New York: Nova Science.

Efimerida ton Sydakton (2013) Το κρυφό καταστατικό της ναζιστικής οργάνωσης Χ.Α. (The secret constitution of the Nazi Golden Dawn), available at: http://archive.efsyn.gr/?p=123425.

Ellinas, A. (2013) 'The rise of Golden Dawn: The new face of the far right in Greece', *South European Society and Politics*, 18(4): 543–565.

———— (2015 forthcoming) 'Neo-Nazism in an established democracy: The persistence of Golden Dawn in Greece', *South European Society and Politics*, doi: 10.1080/13608746.2014.981379.

Ellwood, S. (1995) 'The extreme right in Spain', in Cheles, L., Ferguson, R. and Vaughan, M. (eds.) *The Extreme Right in Western and Eastern Europe*. London and New York: Longman.

EU Observer (2014) 'Greece's Golden Dawn seeks allies in EP', available at: http://euobserver.com/eu-elections/124170.

Eurostat (2014) Unemployment rate by sex and age groups—annual average, %,, available at: http://appsso.eurostat.ec.europa.eu/nui/show.do?dataset=une_rt_a&lang=en.

Featherstone, K. (2005) 'Introduction: "Modernisation" and the structural constraints of Greek politics', *West European Politics*, 28(2): 223–241.

Ferrari, S. and Cribari-Neto, F. (2004) 'Beta regression for modelling rates and proportions', *Journal of Applied Statistics*, 31(7): 799–815.

DOI: 10.1057/9781137535917.0012

Ford, R. and Goodwin, M. (2010) 'Angry white men: Individual and contextual predictors of support for the British National Party', *Political Studies*, 58(1): 1–25.

——— (2014) *Revolt on the Right: Explaining Support for the Radical Right in Britain*. Oxon: Routledge.

Fragoudaki, A. (1997) 'The political consequences of the a historical portrayal of the Greek nation', in Anna Fragoudaki, and Thalia Dragona (eds.) *What is our Homeland? Ethnocentrism in Education*. Athens: Alexandria: 143–198.

——— (2013) *Ο εθνικισμός και η άνοδος της ακροδεξιάς* (Nationalism and the rise of the extreme right). Athens: Aleaxandria.

Fragoudaki, A. and Dragona, T (eds.) (1997) *Τι Είναι η Πατρίδα μας; Εθνοκεντρισμός στην Εκπαίδευση* (What is our homeland? Ethnocentrism in education). Athens: Alexandria.

Gallagher, M., Laver, M. and Mair, P. (2006) *Representative Government in Modern Europe*. New York: McGraw-Hill.

Gellner, E. (1983) *Nations and Nationalism*. Oxford: Blackwell.

Gemenis, K. (2010) 'Winning votes and weathering storms: The 2009 European and parliamentary elections in Greece', *Representation*, 46(3): 353–362.

Georgiadou, V. (2011) 'Glissement des partis d'extrême droite vers le centre et renouvellement de l'extrêmisme à leur marge', *Revue des Sciences Sociales*, 46: 36–45.

——— (2013) 'Greece', in Melzer, R. and Serafin, S. (eds.) *Right-Wing Extremism in Europe: Counter-Strategies and Labor-Market Oriented Exit Strategies*. Friedrich Ebert Foundation.

Givens, T. (2004) 'The radical right gender gap', *Comparative Political Studies*, 37(1): 30–54

Golder, M. (2003) 'Explaining variation in the success of extreme right parties in Western Europe', *Comparative Political Studies*, 36 (4): 432–466.

Goodwin, M. (2011) *New British Fascism: Rise of the British National Party*. Oxon: Routledge.

Griffin, R. (1991) *The Nature of Fascism*. London: Routledge.

——— (2004) 'Introduction: God's counterfeiters? Investigating the triad of fascism, totalitarianism and (political) religion', *Totalitarian Movements and Political Religions*, 5(3): 291–325.

Gurr, R. (1970) *Why Men Rebel*. Princeton, NJ: Princeton University Press.

DOI: 10.1057/9781137535917.0012

Hainsworth, P. (2008) *The Extreme Right in Western Europe*. Milton Park, Abingdon, Oxon and New York: Routledge.

Halikiopoulou, D. (2011) *Patterns of Secularization: Church, State and Nation in Greece and the Republic of Ireland*. Farnham: Ashgate.

Halikiopoulou, D., Mock, S. and Vasilopoulou, S. (2013) 'The civic zeitgeist: nationalism and liberal values in the European radical right', *Nations and Nationalism*, 19(1): 107–127.

Halikiopoulou, D., Nanou, K. and Vasilopoulou, S. (2012) 'The paradox of nationalism: The common denominator of radical right and radical left Euroscepticism', *European Journal of Political Research*, 51(4): 504–539.

Hasapopoulos, N. (2013) *Χρυσή Αυγή - Η Ιστορία, τα Πρόσωπα και η Αλήθεια* (Golden Dawn: The history, the people and the truth). Athens: Livanis.

Hechter, M. (2000) *Containing Nationalism*. Oxford: Oxford University Press.

Human Rights Watch (2013) 'Greece: Abusive crackdown on migrants', available at: http://www.hrw.org/news/2013/06/12/greece-abusive-crackdown-migrants.

Ignazi, P. (1992) 'The silent counter-revolution: Hypotheses on the emergence of extreme right-wing parties in Europe', *European Journal of Political Research*, 22: 3–34.

Kaldor, M. (2004) 'Nationalism and globalization', *Nations and Nationalism*, 10(1/2): 161–177.

Kalyvas, S.N. and Marantzidis, N. (2002) 'Greek communism, 1968–2001', *East European Politics and Societies*, 16(3): 655–690.

Kathimerini (2013) 'The results of operation "Hospitable Zeus" for the past six months have been released' (Ανακοινώθηκαν τα αποτελέσματα της επιχείρησης «Ξένιος Ζευς» των τελευταίων έξι μηνών), 6 February, available at: http://www.kathimerini.gr/4dcgi/_w_articles_kathremote_1_06/02/2013_482280.

——— (2014) 'Δύο δεκαετίες επιθέσεων της Χρυσής Αυγής' (Two decades of Golden Dawn assaults), available at: http://www.kathimerini.gr/791530/article/epikairothta/politikh/dyo-dekaeties-epi8esewn-ths-xryshs-ayghs.

Katsourides, Y. (2013) 'Determinants of extreme right reappearance in Cyprus: The National Popular Front (ELAM), Golden Dawn's sister party', *South European Society and Politics*, 18(4): 567–589.

DOI: 10.1057/9781137535917.0012

Kaufmann, D., Kraay, A. and Mastruzzi, M. (2010) 'The worldwide governance indicators: Methodology and analytical issues', World Bank Policy Research Working Paper No. 5430, available at SSRN: http://ssrn.com/abstract=1682130.

Kaufmann, E. (2002) 'Modern formation, ethnic reformation: The social sources of the American nation', *Geopolitics*, 7(2): 98–120.

Kitschelt, H. (2007) 'Growth and persistence of the radical right in postindustrial democracies: Advances and challenges in comparative research', *West European Politics*, 30(5): 1176–1206.

Kitschelt, H. and McGann, A. (1995) *The Radical Right in Western Europe: A Comparative Analysis*. Ann Arbor: University of Michigan Press.

Kohn, H. (1946) *The Idea of Nationalism: A Study in Its Origins and Background*. New York: Macmillan.

Koopmans, R. and Statham, P. (1999) 'Ethnic and civic conceptions of nationhood and the differential success of the extreme right in Germany and Italy', in Giugni, M., McAdam, D. and Tilly, C. (eds.) *How Social Movements Matter*. Minneapolis: University of Minnesota Press, pp. 225–251.

Koulouri, C. (ed.) (2002) *Clio in the Balkans: The Politics of History Education*. Centre for Democracy and Reconciliation in Southeast Europe, Thessaloniki.

Kriesi, H., Grande, E., Lachat, R., Dolezal, M., Bornschier, S. and Frey, T. (2006) 'Globalisation and transformation of the national political space: Six European countries compared', *European Journal of Political Research*, 45(6): 921–956.

——— (2008) *West European Politics in the Age of Globalization*. Cambridge: Cambridge University Press.

Linz, J. (1976) 'Some notes toward a comparative study of fascism in sociological historical perspective', in Laqueur, W. (ed.) *Fascisim: A Reader's Guide*. Berkeley: University of California Press.

Lipset, S.M. (1960) *Political Man: The Social Bases of Politics*. New York: Doubleday.

Lubbers, M., Gijberts, M. and Scheepers, P. (2002) 'Extreme right-wing voting in Western Europe', *European Journal of Political Research*, 41: 345–378.

Lubbers, M. and Scheepers, P. (2002) 'French front national voting: A micro and macro perspective', *Ethnic and Racial Studies*, 25(1): 120–149.

DOI: 10.1057/9781137535917.0012

References 97

Lucassen, G. and Lubbers, M. (2011) 'Who fears what? Explaining far-right-wing preference in Europe by distinguishing perceived cultural and economic ethnic threats', *Comparative Political Studies*, 45(5): 547–574.

Lyrintzis, C. and Nikolakopoulos, H. (2004) 'The political system and elections in Greece', About Greece, 2nd edn, Greek Ministry of Press and Mass Media, Athens, available at: video.minpress.gr/../aboutgreece/aboutgreece_political_system.pdf.

Mann, M. (2004) *Fascists*. Cambridge: Cambridge University Press.

Marchi, R. (2013) Portugal. In R. Melzer & Serafin, S. (Eds.), *Right-wing extremism in Europe: Counter-strategies and Labor-Market Oriented Exit Strategies*. Friedrich Ebert Foundation.

Marvin, C. and Ingle, D.W. (1998) *Blood Sacrifice and the Nation: Totem Rituals and the American Flag*. Cambridge: Cambridge University Press.

Mayer, N. (1999) *Ces Francais Qui Votent FN* (These French people who vote National Front). Paris: Flammarion.

—— (2013) 'From Jean-Marie to Marine Le Pen: Electoral change on the far right', *Parliamentary Affairs*, 66(1): 160–178.

Michaloliakos, N. (2013) Interview with SKAI, available at: https://www.youtube.com/watch?v=uE-Cttc99UE.

Minkenberg, M. (2000) 'The renewal of the radical right: between modernity and antimodernity', *Government and Opposition*, 35(2): 170–188.

Mitsopoulos, M. and Pelagidis, T. (2011) *Understanding the Crisis in Greece: From Boom to Bust*. Basingstoke: Palgrave Macmillan.

Mouzelis, N. and Pagoulatos, G. (2002) 'Civil society and citizenship in postwar Greece', Athens University of Economics and Business, available at: http://www.aueb.gr/users/ pagoulatos/mouzelis%20 civil%20society.pdf.

Mudde, C. (2007) *Populist Radical Right Parties in Europe*. Cambridge and New York: Cambridge University Press.

—— (2010) 'The Populist Radical Right: A Pathological Normalcy', *West European Politics*, 33(6): 1167–1186.

Nairn, T. (1975) 'The modern Janus', *New Left Review*, 1(94): 3–29.

Nolte, E. (1965) *Three Faces of Fascism*. London: Weidenfeld & Nicolson.

Norris, P. (2005) *Radical Right: Voter and Parties in the Electoral Market*. Cambridge: Cambridge University Press.

DOI: 10.1057/9781137535917.0012

Pappas, T. (2003) 'The transformation of the Greek party system since 1951', *West European Politics*, 26(2): 90–114.

—— (2013) 'Why Greece failed', *Journal of Democracy*, 24(2): 31–45.

—— (2014) *Populism and Crisis Politics in Greece*. Basingstoke: Palgrave Pivot.

Pappas, T. and O'Malley, E. (2014) 'Civil compliance and "political Luddism": Explaining variance in social unrest during crisis in Ireland and Greece', *American Behavioral Scientist*, 58(12): 1592–1613.

Payne, S. (1980) *Fascism: Comparison and Definition*. Madison: University of Wisconsin Press.

Psarras, D. (2012) *Η Μαύρη Βίβλος της Χρυσής Αυγής, Ντοκουμέντα από την ιστορία και τη δράση μιας ναζιστικής ομάδας* (The Black Bible of the Golden Dawn: The documented history of a Nazi group). Athens: Polis.

Psychogios, Dimitris. 2013. *Η πολιτική βία στην Ελληνική κοινωνία* [Political violence in Greek society], 2nd edition. Thessaloniki: Epikedro.

Public Issue (2012) 'Το κριτήριο ψήφου στις εκλογές της 17ης Ιουνίου 2012. Οι λόγοι για τους οποίους οι ψηφοφόροι επέλεξαν το κόμμα τους' (Voting criteria for the June 2012 elections. The reasons behind voters' party choice), published 19 June, available at: http://www.publicissue.gr/2039/criterion/.

Reif, K. and Schmitt, H. (1980) 'Nine second-order national elections: A conceptual framework for the analysis of European election results', *European Journal of Political Research*, 8(1): 3–44.

Rippeyoung, P. (2007) 'When women are right: The influence of gender, work and values on European far right party support', *International Feminist Journal of Politics*, 9(3): 379–397.

Rydgren, J. (2007) 'The sociology of the radical right', *The Annual Review of Sociology*, 33: 241–262.

—— (2008) 'Immigration sceptics, xenophobes or racists? Radical right-wing voting in six West European countries', *European Journal of Political Research*, 47: 737–765.

—— (ed.) (2013) *Class Politics and the Radical Right*. Oxon: Routledge.

Smith, A.D. (1991) *National Identity*. London: Penguin.

—— (1992) 'Chosen peoples: Why ethnic groups survive', *Ethnic and Racial Studies*, 15(3): 436–456.

DOI: 10.1057/9781137535917.0012

———— (1999) 'Ethnic election and national destiny: Some religious origins of nationalist ideals', *Nations and Nationalism*, 5(3): 331–355.

———— (2000) 'The sacred dimension of nationalism', *Millenium Special Issue: Religion and International Relations*, 29(3): 791–814.

———— (2003) *Chosen Peoples: Sacred Sources of National Identity*. Oxford: Oxford University Press.

Ta Nea (2011) 'Με 155 «ναι» ψηφίστηκε το Μεσοπρόθεσμο' (The midterm fiscal strategy plan was approved by 155 'in favour'), 29 June, available at: http://www.tanea.gr/ellada/article/?aid=4638591.

———— (2012) 'Indictment for "blasphemous" pastitios"' (Στο σκαμνί για το «βλάσφημο» παστίτσιο) 26 September, available at: http://www.tanea.gr/news/greece/article/4754703/?iid=2.

To Vima (2011) 'Δημοψήφισμα: «Ναι» ή «όχι» στη νέα δανειακή σύμβαση' (Referendum: 'Yes' or 'No' to the new loan agreement), 31 October, available at: http://www.tovima.gr/politics/article/?aid=427794.

———— (2014) 'Εκπαίδευση στα όπλα από τη Χρυσή Αυγή', 10 October, available at: http://www.tovima.gr/society/article/?aid=640009.

Van der Brug, W. and Fennema, M. (2007) 'What causes people to vote for a radical right party? A review of recent work', *International Journal of Public Opinion Research*, 19(4): 474–487.

Van der Brug, W., Fennema, M., De Lange, S. and I. Baller (2013) 'Radical right parties: Their voters and their electoral competitors', in Rydgrn, J. (ed.) *Class Politics and the Radical Right*, Oxon: Routledge.

Vasilopoulou, S. (2011) 'European integration and the radical right: Three patterns of opposition', *Government and Opposition*, 46(2): 223–244.

Vasilopoulou, S. and Halikiopoulou, D. (2013) 'In the shadow of Grexit: The Greek Election of 11 June 2012', *South European Society and Politics*, 18(4): 523–542.

Vasilopoulou, S., Halikiopoulou, D. and Exadaktylos, T. (2014) 'Greece in crisis: Austerity, populism and the politics of blame', *Journal of Common Market Studies*, 52(2): 388–402.

VPRC (2012) 'Βουλευτικές Εκλογές 17ης Ιουνίου 2012 Εκτιμήσεις Εκλογικών Μετατοπίσεων' (17 June 2012 legislative elections: Voters' displacement), survey conducted on 15 June, available at: http://www.vprc.gr/article.php?id=1169.

DOI: 10.1057/9781137535917.0012

Wimmer, A. (1997) 'Explaining xenophobia and racism: A critical review of current research approaches', *Ethnic and Racial Studies*, 20(1): 17–41.

Zimmer, O. (2003) 'Boundary mechanisms and symbolic resources: Towards a process-oriented approach to national identity', *Nations and Nationalism*, 9(2): 173–193.

Golden Dawn Materials

(The materials listed in this section have been accessed during the period between July and December 2014)

Golden Dawn (08/11/2014) 'Η Χρυσή Αυγή στο πλευρό των Ενόπλων Δυνάμεων: Συνάντηση με εκπροσώπους της Ένωσης Αποστράτων Αξιωματικών Στρατού' (The Golden Dawn stands together with the armed forces: A meeting with the representatives of the Union of Retired Army Generals), available at: http://www.xryshaygh. com/enimerosi/view/sunanthsh-me-ekproswpous-ths-enwshs-apostratwn-ajiwmatikwn-stratou.

Golden Dawn (09/10/2014) 'Η Ιδέα του Στρατού' (The idea of the army), available at: http://www.xryshaygh.com/enimerosi/view/h-idea-tou-stratou#ixzz3MdOmyBJR.

Golden Dawn (19/06/2014) 'Ποδόσφαιρο και Ολυμπιακοί Αγώνες' (Football and Olympic Games), available at: http://www.xryshaygh. com/index.php/enimerosi/view/podosfairo-kai-olumpiakoi-agwnes#ixzz3736c8aFw.

Golden Dawn (12/06/2014) 'Οι σκάρτοι - Κείμενο του Γεώργιου Γρίβα Διγενή' (The degenerate—a text by Georgios Grivas Digenis), available at: http://www.xryshaygh.com/enimerosi/view/oi-skartoi-keimeno-tou-gewrgiou-griba-digenh.

Golden Dawn (30/05/2014) 'Η Δίκη του Σωκράτη' (The trial of Socrates), available at: http://www.xryshaygh.com/index.php/ enimerosi/view/h-dikh-tou-swkrath#ixzz37370r6nA.

Golden Dawn (28/05/2014) '29 Μαΐου 1453 «Η Πόλις αλίσκεται»' (29 May 1453—the sacking of Constantinople), available at: http://www. xryshaygh.com/index.php/enimerosi/view/29-maioy-1453-..h-polis-alisketai#ixzz3738F2xHF.

Golden Dawn (27/05/2014) 'Συνεργασία: Τουρκισμός και αριστερισμός' (Cooperation between Turkey and the Left), available at: http://

DOI: 10.1057/9781137535917.0012

www.xryshaygh.com/index.php/enimerosi/view/tourkismos-kai-aristerismos#ixzz3738PJc8U.

Golden Dawn (23/05/2014) 'Σμηναγός Κωνσταντίνος Ηλιάκης: Αθάνατος!' (Captain Konstantinos Eliakis: Immortal!), available at: http://www.xryshaygh.com/index.php/enimerosi/view/smhnagos-kwnstantinos-hliakhs-athanatos#ixzz3738djpXM.

Golden Dawn (13/05/2014) 'Κουτσούφλιανη 13 Μαΐου 1898: Ένα πραγματικό Ελληνικό Ολοκαύτωμα' (Koutsofliani 13 May 1898: A Greek Holocaust), available at: http://www.xryshaygh.com/index.php/enimerosi/view/koutsouflianh-13-maiou-1898-ena-pragmatiko-ellhniko-olokautwma#ixzz373972yhP.

Golden Dawn (09/04/2014) 'Άγνωστες μορφές του Ελληνισμού: Γεώργιος Δουράτσος' (Unknown figures of Helenism: Georgios Douratsos), available at: http://www.xryshaygh.com/index.php/enimerosi/view/agnwstes-morfes-tou-ellhnismou-gewrgios-douratsos#ixzz373BVKCJc.

Golden Dawn (08/04/2014) 'Το Μαύρο Πάσχα των Ελλήνων της Θράκης - 6 Απριλίου 1914' (The Black Easter of the Greeks of Trace—6 April 1914), available at: http://www.xryshaygh.com/index.php/enimerosi/view/to-mauro-pascha-twn-ellhnwn-ths-thrakhs-6-apriliou-1914#ixzz373BaJwGR.

Golden Dawn (06/04/2014) '6 Απριλίου 1941: Το δεύτερο «ΟΧΙ» των Ελλήνων' (6 April 1941: The second NO of the Greeks), available at: http://www.xryshaygh.com/index.php/enimerosi/view/6-apriliou-to-deutero-ochi-twn-ellhnwn-h-epopoiia-ths-grammhs-metaja#ixzz373Bl6v7r.

Golden Dawn (25/03/2014) '25η Μαρτίου 1821: Όπως τότε έτσι και σήμερα όλοι εναντίον μας' (25 March 1821: As in the past everyone is against us today), available at: http://www.xryshaygh.com/enimerosi/view/25h-martiou-1821-opws-tote-etsi-kai-shmera-oloi-enantion-mas.

Golden Dawn (17/03/2014) 'Διακήρυξη Ελευθερίας: 17 Μαρτίου 1821 - Η Αυγή της Επανάστασης' (Declaration of Freedom: 17 March 1821—the dawn of the revolution), available at: http://www.xryshaygh.com/index.php/enimerosi/view/diakhruj-eleutherias-17-martiou-1821-h-augh-ths-epanastashs#ixzz373F37Kko.

Golden Dawn (14/03/2014) 'Του ανδρειωμένου ο θάνατος, θάνατος δεν λογιέται: Στο πάνθεον των Ηρώων ο Ευαγόρας Παλληκαρίδης' (The death of a brave man may not be considered death: Evagoras Pallikarides joins the Pantheon of Heroes), available at: http://www.xryshaygh.

DOI: 10.1057/9781137535917.0012

com/index.php/enimerosi/view/tou-antreiwmenou-euagora-h-thusia#ixzz373FFRU4G.

Golden Dawn (27/02/2014) 'Σαν σήμερα το 1943 περνά στην αιωνιότητα ο Εθνικός μας ποιητής Κωστής Παλαμάς' (On this date in 1943, our national poet Kostis Palamas passes on to eternity), available at: http://www.xryshaygh.com/index.php/enimerosi/view/san-shmera-to-1943-perna-sthn-aiwniothta-o-ethnikos-mas-poihths-kwsths-pala#ixzz373G3qNZs.

Golden Dawn (25/02/2014) 'Αρχαιοελληνικός χαιρετισμός: Για να «μαθαίνει» η ψοφοδεξιά του Βορίδη και η αντεθνική αριστερά' (Ancient Greek salute for the information of Vorides's degenerate right and the antinational left), available at: http://www.xryshaygh.com/index.php/enimerosi/view/archaioellhnikos-chairetismos-gia-na-mathainei-h-psofodejia-tou-boridh-kai#ixzz373GQS2a1.

Golden Dawn (02/02/2014) 'Σαν σήμερα γεννήθηκε ο τραγικά επίκαιρος Γεώργιος Σουρής' (This date marks the birth of the tragically timely Georgios Souris), available at: http://www.xryshaygh.com/index.php/enimerosi/view/san-shmera-gennhthhke-o-tragika-epikairos-gewrgios-sourhs#ixzz373I8YpuN.

Golden Dawn (29/01/2014) 'Σαν σήμερα περνά στην αιωνιότητα ο Κυβερνήτης των «ΟΧΙ», Ιωάννης Μεταξάς' (On this date Ioannis Metaxas, the commander of the NO, passes on to eternity), available at: http://www.xryshaygh.com/enimerosi/view/san-shmera-perna-sthn-aiwniothta-o-kubernhths-twn-ochi-iwannhs-metajas.

Golden Dawn (09/01/2014) 'Μαρτύρων και Ηρώων Αίμα: Γεωργάλλας Μιχαήλ' (Blood of martyrs and heroes: Georgalas Mihael), available at: http://www.xryshaygh.com/index.php/enimerosi/view/marturwn-kai-hrwwn-aima-gewrgallas-michahl#ixzz373KKXCis.

Golden Dawn (07/01/2014) 'Εφημερίδα "Ακρόπολις": Ο απερχόμενος δήμαρχος απαγόρευσε στους βουλευτές της Χρυσής Αυγής να μπουν στο λιμάνι' (Newspaper Acropolis: The former mayor prohibited Golden Dawn MPs to enter the port), available at: http://www.xryshaygh.com/enimerosi/view/efhmerida-akropolis-o-aperchomenos-dhmarchos-apagoreuse-stous-bouleutes-ths.

Golden Dawn (05/01/2014) 'Σαν σήμερα 5 Ιανουαρίου 1913: Η θριαμβευτική ναυμαχία της Λήμνου' (On this date 5 January 1913: The triumphant battle of Lemnos), available at: http://www.xryshaygh.com/enimerosi/view/san-shmera-5-ianouariou-1913-h-thriambeutikh-naumachia-ths-lhmnou.

DOI: 10.1057/9781137535917.0012

Golden Dawn (03/01/2014) '3 Ιανουαρίου 1911: Σαν σήμερα περνά στην αιωνιότητα ο "κοσμοκαλόγερος" Αλέξανδρος Παπαδιαμάντης' (3 January 1911: On this date Alexandros Papadiamantis passes on to eternity), available at: http://www.xryshaygh.com/enimerosi/view/3-ianouariou-1911-san-shmera-perna-sthn-aiwniothta-o-kosmokalogeros-alejand.

Golden Dawn (27/12/2013) 'Μαύρη μέρα – Σαν σήμερα ξεκινά η λειτουργία του ΔΝΤ' (Black day—on this day the IMF begins its operations), available at: http://www.xryshaygh.com/enimerosi/view/maurh-mera-san-shmera-jekina-h-leitourgia-tou-dnt.

Golden Dawn (04/12/2013) Όλη η αλήθεια για τον "κόκκινο Δεκέμβρη" του 44' (The truth about the red December of 1944), available at: http://www.xryshaygh.com/index.php/enimerosi/view/olh-h-alhtheia-gia-ton-kokkino-dekembrh-tou-441#ixzz373NpOkRb.

Golden Dawn (25/11/2013) 'Πίνδαρος «Ο Εκλεκτός των Μουσών» - Α' Μέρος' (Pindar: The chosen of the muses—Part A), available at: http://www.xryshaygh.com/index.php/enimerosi/view/pindaros-o-eklektos-twn-mouswn-a-meros#ixzz373OSaQ9n.

Golden Dawn (22/11/2013) '22 Νοεμβρίου 1940: «Στο βάθος μακριά, προβάλει η Κορυτσά…!»' (22 November 1940: Koritsa is at the end of the road), available at: http://www.xryshaygh.com/index.php/enimerosi/view/sto-bathos-makria-probalei-h-korutsa#ixzz373OY7FXf.

Golden Dawn (20/11/2013a) '«Ύβρις»: Το μέγα σφάλμα που ποτέ δεν μένει ατιμώρητο' (Hubris: The great mistake that cannot go unpunished), available at: http://www.xryshaygh.com/enimerosi/view/ubris-to-mega-sfalma-pou-pote-den-menei-atimwrhto.

Golden Dawn (20/11/2013b) 'Χοσέ Αντόνιο Πρίμο ντε Ριβέρα: Παρών! Το παρελθόν οδηγεί τα βήματά μας στο μέλλον!' (Hose Antonio Primo de Rivera: Present! The past guides our steps to the future!), available at: http://www.xryshaygh.com/enimerosi/view/chose-antonio-primo-nte-ribera-parwnto-parelthon-odhgei-ta-bhmata-mas-sto-m.

Golden Dawn (19/11/2013) 'Κυριάκος Μάτσης - Ήρωας ΕΟΚΑ: «Ου περί χρημάτων τον αγώνα ποιούμεθα αλλά περί αρετής»' (Kyriakos Matsis—a hero of EOKA: We do not fight for money, we fight for virtue), available at: http://www.xryshaygh.com/index.php/enimerosi/view/kuriakos-matshs-hrwas-eoka-ou-peri-chrhmatwn-ton-agwna-poioumetha-alla-peri#ixzz373PqQGbV.

DOI: 10.1057/9781137535917.0012

Golden Dawn (12/11/2013) 'Εχετλαίος: Ο πολεμιστής της Μάχης του Μαραθώνα' (Ehetleos: A soldier in the Battle of Marathon), available at: http://www.xryshaygh.com/index.php/enimerosi/view/echetlaios#ixzz373QIP6Lo.

Golden Dawn (09/11/2013) 'Σαν σήμερα το Ολοκαύτωμα της Μονής Αρκαδίου -"Θρησκευτικός φανατισμός" λένε τα σχολικά βιβλία της ΝΔ' (On this data the Holocaust of the Arkadi Monastery—religious fanaticism say the school of books of ND), available at: http://www.xryshaygh.com/index.php/enimerosi/view/san-shmera-to-olokautwma-ths-monhs-arkadiou-thrhskeutikos-fanatismos-lene-t#ixzz373QXzYCO.

Golden Dawn (30/10/2013) 'Συζητώντας με τον Ι. Δραγούμη, 93 χρόνια μετά' (Conversing with I. Dragoumis, 93 years later), available at: http://www.xryshaygh.com/index.php/enimerosi/view/suzhtwntas-me-ton-i.dragoumh-93-chronia-meta#ixzz373QwZIqy.

Golden Dawn (28/10/2013) '28η Οκτωβρίου 1940: Το υπερήφανο "ΟΧΙ" των Ελλήνων' (28 October 1940: The proud Greek 'NO'), available at: http://www.xryshaygh.com/index.php/enimerosi/view/28h-oktwbriou-1940-to-uperhfano-ochi-twn-ellhnwn#ixzz373RCwnU8.

Golden Dawn (13/10/2013) '29 Μαρτίου 1870–13 Οκτωβρίου 1904: Παύλος Μελάς - Ο Ελευθερωτής της Μακεδονίας' (29 March 1870–13 October 1904: Pavlos Melas—the Liberator of Macedonia), available at: http://www.xryshaygh.com/index.php/enimerosi/view/29-martiou-1870–13-oktwbriou-1904-paulos-melas-o-eleutherwths-ths-makedonia#ixzz373WCjNFH.

Golden Dawn (25/09/2013) '25 Σεπτεμβρίου 1849: Ο Νικηταράς ο Τουρκοφάγος περνά στο πάνθεον των Ηρώων του Έθνους' (25 September 1849: Nikitaras the Turk-eater joins the Nation's pantheon of Heroes), available at: http://www.xryshaygh.com/index.php/enimerosi/view/25-septembriou-1849-o-nikhtaras-o-tourkofagos-perna-sto-pantheon-twn-hrwwn#ixzz373WjoDN8.

Golden Dawn (15/09/2013) '15 Σεπτεμβρίου 1944: Ντοκουμέντα και μαρτυρίες για την κομμουνιστική θηριωδία' (15 September 1944: Documenting the communist atrocity), available at: http://www.xryshaygh.com/enimerosi/view/15-septembriou-1944-h-kommounistikh-thhriwdia-ston-meligala.

Golden Dawn (04/09/2013) 'Η μάχη στο Σαγγάριο ποταμό: 10 Αυγούστου - 4 Σεπτεμβρίου 1921' (The battle at Saggarios rivier: 10

DOI: 10.1057/9781137535917.0012

August–4 September 1921), available at: http://www.xryshaygh.com/enimerosi/view/h-machh-sto-saggario-potamo-10-augoustou-4-septembriou-1921.

Golden Dawn (29/08/2013) '29 Αυγούστου 1949: Η ημέρα της πολεμικής αρετής των Ελλήνων στο Γράμμο – Βίτσι' (29 August 1949: The day of the Greeks excelled at Grammos—Vitsi), available at: http://www.xryshaygh.com/enimerosi/view/h-hmera-ths-polemikhs-areths-twn-ellhnwn-29-augoustou-1949-grammos-bitsi.

Golden Dawn (19/08/2013) 'Στις αμμουδιές του Ομήρου' (In Homer's tails), available at: http://www.xryshaygh.com/enimerosi/view/stis-ammoudies-tou-omhrou.

Golden Dawn (12/08/2013) 'Ο Μύθος του Περσέα και της Μέδουσας' (The Myth of Perseus and Medusa), available at: http://www.xryshaygh.com/enimerosi/view/o-muthos-tou-persea-kai-ths-medousas.

Golden Dawn (06/08/2013) 'Οι ξεχασμένοι, οι "δεύτεροι" και οι πραγματικοί άνθρωποι του πνεύματος' (The forgotten, the 'secondary' and the true men of spirit), available at: http://www.xryshaygh.com/enimerosi/view/oi-jechasmenoi-oi-deuteroi-kai-oi-pragmatikoi-anthrwpoi-tou-pneumatos.

Golden Dawn (2/08/2013) 'Συνεργασία: Όταν ανεύθυνοι, άνανδροι ή αγύρτες υμνούν δολοφόνους' (Cooperation: When cowardly irresponsible men glorify murder), available at: http://www.xryshaygh.com/enimerosi/view/sunergasia-otan-aneuthunoi-anandroi-h-agurtes-umnoun-dolofonous.

Golden Dawn (01/08/2013) '1 Αυγούστου 1973: Η αυτοκτονία του προδότη κομμουνιστή Νίκου Ζαχαριάδη' (1 August 1973: The suicide of the communist traitor Nikos Zahariades), available at: http://www.xryshaygh.com/enimerosi/view/1-augoustou-1973-h-autoktonia-tou-prodoth-kommounisth-nikou-zachariadh.

Golden Dawn (31/07/2013) 'Μνήμη Ίωνος Δραγούμη: 31 Ιουλίου 1920 - 31 Ιουλίου 2013' (In memory of Ion Dragoumis: 31 July 1920–31 July 2013), available at: http://www.xryshaygh.com/enimerosi/view/mnhmh-iwnos-dragoumh-31-iouliou-1920–31-iouliou-2013.

Golden Dawn (15/07/2013) 'Ισοκράτης, ο πνευματικός πατέρας του Έθνους' (Isocrates, the spiritual leader of the Nation), available at: http://www.xryshaygh.com/enimerosi/view/isokraths-o-pneumatikos-pateras-tou-ethnous.

DOI: 10.1057/9781137535917.0012

Golden Dawn (14/07/2013) 'Ποτέ πια! Οι θηριωδίες των κομμουνιστών στον Φενεό το 1944' (Never again! Communist atrocities at Feneos 1944), available at: http://www.xryshaygh.com/enimerosi/view/pote-pia.

Golden Dawn (01/05/2013) 'Ο Εθνικός Κυβερνήτης Ιωάννης Μεταξάς και η Εργατική Πρωτομαγιά' (National Leader Ioannis Metaxas and Labour Day), available at: http://www.xryshaygh.com/enimerosi/view/o-iwannhs-metajas-kai-h-ergatikh-prwtomagia.

Golden Dawn (06/03/2013) 'Συνεργασία: Πώς αντιμετώπιζε το κράτος τους οφειλέτες του Δημοσίου πριν έναν αιώνα και τώρα' (Cooperation: How the state dealt with public sector debtors today and a century ago), available at: http://www.xryshaygh.com/enimerosi/view/ofeiletes-dhmosiou.

Golden Dawn (05/12/2012) 'Κοινωνικό πρόγραμμα Χρυσής Αυγής "Έλληνες Γιατροί"' (Golden Dawn's social programme 'Greek Doctors'), available at: http://www.xryshaygh.com/enimerosi/view/koinwniko-programma-chrushs-aughs-giatroi-me-sunora#ixzz3MG8fZveR.

Golden Dawn (28/10/2012) 'Μύθοι και αλήθειες για την 28η Οκτωβρίου' (Myths and truths about 28 October), available at: http://www.xryshaygh.com/enimerosi/view/muthoi-kai-alhtheies-gia-thn-28h-oktwbriou.

Golden Dawn (28/09/2012) 'Δουλειά στους Έλληνες από την Χρυσή Αυγή' (Employment for Greeks from the Golden Dawn), available at: http://www.xryshaygh.com/enimerosi/view/o.a.e.d.-ellhnwn-apo-thn-chrush-augh.

Golden Dawn (04/08/2012) '4η Αυγούστου 1936 – Αφιέρωμα' (In memory of 4 August 1936), available at: http://www.xryshaygh.com/enimerosi/view/4h-augoustou-1936-afierwma.

Golden Dawn (2012a) 'Ιδεολογία' (Ideology), available at: http://www.xryshaygh.com/kinima/ideologia.

Golden Dawn (2012b) 'Ταυτότητα' (Identity), available at: http://www.xryshaygh.com/index.php/kinima.

Golden Dawn (2012c) 'Θέσεις' (Positions), available at: http://www.xryshaygh.com/kinima/thesis.

Golden Dawn (2012d) 'Χρυσή Αυγή: Ένα κίνημα ιδεολογικό' (Golden Dawn: An ideological movement), available at: http://www.xryshaygh.com/assets/files/ideologia.pdf.

Indexes

General Index

ANEL, 24, 25, 40

British National Party (BNP), 35, 42
Byzantine Empire, 10, 62, 70, 71, 72–73
Byzantium, see Byzantine Empire

clientelism, 26, 80
Coalition of the Radical Left, see SYRIZA
Communist Party of Greece, see KKE
Communist Youth of Greece, see KNE
Corpus Christi (play), 84–85
crisis, 5, 8–9, 11, 13, 16, 22–23, 23–29, 30, 35, 39, 48–49, 51, 53, 65, 76, 77, 79–81, 82, 86, 87
  economic, 7, 8, 11, 16, 22–26, 28, 29, 51, 56, 79–81, 88
  of the nation or of the nation-state, 5, 9–11, 16, 28, 29, 30, 51, 68
Cyprus, 8, 62, 70, 72, 87

demand side, see explanations, demand-side

Democratic Left, see DIMAR
DIMAR, 25, 40
Discourse Opportunity Structures (DOS), see opportunity stuctures, discourse

EES, 12, 33, 37–39, 47
ELAM, 8, 72, 88
elections, 4, 13, 16–17, 20–23, 40, 42, 79
  European, 2, 5, 11, 18–19, 32, 37, 46–47, 79
  local, 11, 17–18, 20
  municipal, 17–18, 19, 20
  national, 2, 11, 18–19, 24–25, 32, 33, 37
EPEN, 17, 20
ethnic election, 9, 10–11, 13, 14, 65, 68, 69, 70–71, 77
European Election Study, see EES
European Union, 23, 36–7, 44, 46, 47–48, 60, 63
explanations
  demand-side 6–7, 11, 13, 16, 79, 87
  supply-side 6, 7–8, 11, 13, 16, 51–63, 79, 80, 87
extreme right, see Far right

DOI: 10.1057/9781137535917.0013

Index of individuals

Note: an asterisk indicates a member or former member of the Golden Dawn

Frequently cited authors

DOI: 10.1057/9781137535917.0013

DOI: 10.1057/9781137535917.0013